What people are saying...

This book is a story about transformation. It's the perfect example of God's intent for Troy's life and satan's intent to keep him ensnared in order to destroy his marriage, children, finances, and ultimately his life. Troy was a man deep in a spiraling lifestyle that God's love transformed into a man he did not even want to be. Troy went from a person running hard from God and avoiding at great lengths anyone who talked about God, to one passionately seeking God every waking moment. His true life and purpose is now being fulfilled. As a result of his leading by example, his five children are following in his footsteps with the same passion.

This book will encourage you to trust God for everything – large and small. Let it inspire you to run after God and fulfill the destiny that God has planned for you and your family.

~Richard and Glenda Holcomb
Mentor/Global Awakening Board members

Troy called us shortly after the accident and asked my wife, Sherry, and me to pray for his daughter, Maggie, who was being transported by helicopter at that moment to a San Antonio hospital. We prayed with Troy over the telephone and then continued to pray for the entire Faust family. The miracle testimony Troy shared is 100% true. We have known the Faust family for many years. They don't just believe the Word of God, they live it!

~Max Greiner, Jr., President

D1605614

The Coming King Foundation

Buckle your seat belts, and get ready for a ride... this book is the full meal deal. *The Impossible is Nothing* will encourage you, inspire you, and provoke you with its perspective of who God is and how He works in people today. Troy, who was wild at heart before it ever became a book title, is living proof that when we delight ourselves in the Lord, He gives us the desires of our heart. The stories in this book are true and dramatic. The insights are practical and easy to apply. The impact is profound and real. Now sit back, open up your heart and mind, enjoy the journey, and celebrate the extravagance of God's goodness.

~David Danielson, Pastor
Impact Christian Fellowship

This book is a wonderful story of how the LORD took a man of this world and recreated him as a Man desperate for GOD'S heart. It is a most enjoyable, entertaining and challenging story of the MIRACLES of the Living GOD that broke Troy's heart wide open in answer to his wife's prayers. Troy was left with the conviction that "THE IMPOSSIBLE IS NOTHING with the LORD." He now lives his life demonstrating that truth. You will be blessed and encouraged.

~Franklin & Katie Bess Williamson
Missionaries to Asia / Leadership Team
Impact Christian Fellowship

The Impossible Is Nothing

By Troy Faust

DEDICATION

To my bride. She is my dream girl. She is my single greatest treasure second only to salvation. She and Jesus have something in common; they both make me look alot better than I really am.

ACKNOWLEDGEMENTS

A special thanks to those who made telling the story God wrote in my life possible. Thank you Kathy Behrens, Mark and Beth Eubank, Franklin and Katy Bess Williamson, and Courtney Barton for all your help, encouragement and tireless effort in bringing this about. A special thanks to Richard and Glenda Holcomb for believing when I could not, for picking me up when I fell and for loving me when I was unlovable. I am forever grateful.

TABLE OF CONTENTS

FORWARD

The Impossible Is Nothing is an authentic, heart-warming, yet challenging book. It gives us a fresh look at a loving God, who is pursuing relationship with every person on this planet. Troy Faust invites us into his own journey of a heart that was sought after by God. His encounters and continual pursuit remind us anew how loved we are and how real God is and ready to meet us where we are. Troy's victories over two life-threatening situations in his family illustrate the goodness of God and that the "impossible" is nothing to Him. This book will infuse your faith! I'm so glad that Troy put these stories into print.

~Bill Johnson, Bethel Church, Redding, CA
Author of *When Heaven Invades Earth* and *Hosting the Presence*

The Faust Family are an amazing and wonderful dynasty, a bit like the Duck Dynasty in many ways, but in a Texas setting. In the midst of selling cars, hunting and bowfishing for Alligator gar, this is a family who will pray for you at the drop of a hat. And you will not escape without hearing about the Love of Jesus and the power of God.

I met Troy while on a hunting trip with Bill Johnson, and right away fell in love with his exuberance and passion for life, not to mention his dedication and devotion to his wife and children. But trumping it all, however, is his love for the Lord and for all things pertaining to the Kingdom of God. And with good reason!

You will laugh and cry as you hear the story of Troy's stunning conversion, and then the drama of his daughter's tragic accident. It is so amazing how prevailing prayer and the wonders of God brought this family, and community face to face with an outstanding verifiable miracle.

This book, *The Impossible is Nothing*, will encourage you and perhaps even restore your faith in family, and in God.

~John Arnott,
Catch the Fire, Toronto

MY PRAYER

Lord I need your help.

It is my deep desire to honor You and what You have done for my family and me, to attempt to testify of Your ridiculous mercy and favor that we enjoy. I believe You're calling me to put into print our story but I have no idea what I'm doing. However, I rest in the fact that you do.

Lord, You know the extent of my writing has been love letters and poems to my bride on her birthday and Valentine's Day. It takes a lot of trial and error to get my thoughts out of my head and onto paper. It helps that Michelle is so amazing and incredible and tailor-made for me. She is my greatest treasure second only to salvation. It is with this same motivation that I feel the boldness to undertake this adventure. You are so incredibly amazing to me that I am in constant awe of You. Your mercy and love for me is completely unreasonable and frankly, doesn't make any rational sense. Your goodness overwhelms me and I have come to realize that You are more focused and excited about our future than we are.

Not that You are forgetful Lord, but I feel the

need to remind You of the time a few Father's Days ago I found myself alone at home, and decided in that rare quiet moment, to write a love letter to You. However, when I began to write I suddenly remembered the scripture in Proverbs 15:3 speaking of Your omniscience, *"The eyes of the Lord are in all places seeing all the good and evil that man does."* Nothing escapes Your eye. So I thought, what's the point of writing a letter to You when You know its content even before I write it? Then it occurred to me, I wonder what would happen if I asked You not to look? I mean, would that really work? Is there any scriptural precedent for such a request? Maybe no one has ever thought to ask? So I prayed to You, my omniscient God and asked You not to look over my shoulder as I wrote. I said that I wanted to write You a love letter from my heart to Yours, and I wanted it to be special.

I will never forget Your response to me. It was a resounding 'yes'! I could sense Your excitement in my idea. My thoughts were invaded by a picture of an expectant father waiting to see his firstborn child, pacing back and forth with excitement! The gravity of my request began to sink in, and I knew that it was an important moment in our relationship, pregnant with growth and opportunity. Had I just asked the God of all, not to help me? Wow! (I'm a smart one)! I mean, I know I'm not the sharpest tool in the shed, but this was ridiculous. But, I did it anyway, and You loved it.

I know it would have been a much better letter if I had asked the Holy Spirit to help me, but I wouldn't change it if I could. It has become one of my favorite memories. It belongs to You and me. But Lord, this isn't, I repeat (isn't), the same thing. I am asking for Your help to write this book. So, please feel free to look over my shoulder, invade my thoughts, arrest my attention and give me abilities that I didn't earn.

Thanks, Troy

PREFACE

My wife and I were blessed with four daughters and a son who was born right in the middle. At the time of this writing their ages range from 14 to 24. Our oldest, Megan is married to Cody, a wonderful godly man we have had the pleasure of knowing since he was nine years old. It's been a great joy for my wife and me to see them grow up together and watch the uniqueness of their relationship grow. He was her first boyfriend and she his first girlfriend. Both are involved in our church's youth ministry. They now have two wonderful daughters, which means we are the proud grandparents of two perfect grandchildren. No one told us how much fun being grandparents would be. I've heard it said that if I would've known how much fun grandchildren were, I would have had them first.

Our second daughter Hannah is currently a student at Texas Tech University. Hannah has the sunniest personality of anyone I've ever met. It's contagious. Every day is a new adventure for her. She's one of those people who has never met a stranger. She is now engaged to be married to a young man named Garret who in the short time we have known him, has stolen our hearts. He's a perfect fit for our daughter. But more importantly he's made a decision to be in relationship with our Lord Jesus Christ. It's a huge, overwhelming blessing to see the choices all of our children are making and the caliber of people the Lord is drawing into their lives.

Our son Matt is also a Texas Tech student pursuing a political science degree. He is 20 years old and is in a relationship with a wonderful young lady. He would use "perfect" young lady. To say she is beautiful would be an understatement, but the most beautiful thing about her is her relationship with the Lord. One day my son said, "I know one thing for sure about my relationship with Rachel." "What's that son?" I asked. He replied, "I know I'm number two in her life, and she doesn't mind reminding me." Rachel's stock immediately went up with his statement. Matt loves the Lord deeply, and he doesn't mind showing it. It's beautiful to witness him exercising bravery in daily pursuit of God.

Maggie is our number four child, our third daughter. She's a 17-year-old senior in high school. She is beautiful, vibrant and loves the Lord with all of her heart. She sings and plays the guitar occasionally in our youth group band at church. She has a unique way about her. Though more of a private person, she can be very public at times. I would describe her relationship with the Lord as quiet but deep. She stands up for what she believes in, in a beautifully accepting sort of way. People are so drawn to her, it's amazing! God used Maggie's life to radically change my own.

Last, but certainly not least, there's Sam, which is short for Samantha Joy our 14-year-old. She's the baby of the family, but she's no baby. Sam is known around our house as the force to be reckoned with and is known in more than one circle as a friend of God and an enemy of the devil. Her passion for God, who she affectionately calls Papa, is a running theme in her life.

To say it mildly, we are very proud of all five of our children. They have given us a great gift in their own individual ways. They honor us not only by allowing us to be their parents but also to be their friends. It is truly our great honor to walk with them through this life calling them our son and daughters, as well as brother and sisters in Christ. I have come to understand 3 Johns 1:14:

"I have no greater joy than to hear and see my children walking in the truth."

What a joy it is to know that according to Genesis 1:26, my family and I are made in the image of God. So then, in my simple way of thinking, if we want to bring the greatest joy into the heart and mind of God the Almighty, then all we have to do is choose to walk in His truth.

This book is part of our story about learning to walk in the light of His presence, a story of his amazing mercy and grace and His willingness to reach into the mire of my life and pull me out with His perfect hand. It ends with an absolutely incredible story of His healing power and His unreasonable love.

CHAPTER 1

Heart Stopping Phone Call

*For I am convinced that neither death nor life,
neither angels nor demons, neither the present nor
the future, nor any powers, neither height nor
depth, nor anything else in all creation, will be able
to separate us from the love of God that is in Christ
Jesus our Lord. ~**Romans 8:38-39***

It was a typical hot summer afternoon in July. Life was good. No big problems loomed on the horizon and there were no troubles on our radar. As a matter of fact, things were great. My wife, Michelle and I were enjoying the fruits of our labor, and God had blessed us in many, many ways. Since 2004 we have owned a used car lot in a wonderful small town called Kerrville. Kerrville is located about 60 miles northwest of San Antonio, in the Texas Hill Country. If the Hill Country has a drawback, it's the fact that July and August are way too hot for my liking. I've talked to God about His mistake with the temperature, but He refuses to see it my way.

We had all but raised five fantastic kids in

whom we could not possibly be more proud. The dealership was thriving in spite of the biggest economic meltdown since the Great Depression. No one in our family had any physical issues to speak of, except my growing middle-aged midsection that needed some attention.

I have often said that I believe the Lord has taught me more about His father's heart for me through raising children than He has through attending church. Oh, He does it that way too, sometimes. But the longer I know Him the more I have come to believe that not only *can* He use anything and everything to show His heart and love to us, but He *wants* to use anything and everything. It's just how He is. I once thought that if I wanted to know God I needed to go to church more often. Then I began to notice that He wanted to talk to me outside of church as well. How strange, I thought! It was like He wanted to be a part of my everyday life.

As I grew up a little, I came to believe that He was going to use anything and everything to draw me to Him. Wow! I thought, *God will go to amazing lengths to foster a relationship with me*. Me! At this point in my relationship with Him, I have come to know that it's even more than that; I now believe He just can't help himself. It's not so much a planned strategy (although He does a lot of that too) as it is His consuming love He has for all of us. How else can we rationalize some of the crazy things He has taken upon Himself, leaving heaven, the presence of His Father, His deity and power and coming to this fallen world to rescue, retrieve and restore us to Himself? In my immaturity, I once thought we simply had an apple problem. I mean, these people named Adam and Eve that I never knew, screwed up and agreed with the enemy, who promised power through knowledge over the truth. Funny isn't it? He is truth and we know that truth is knowledge and knowledge is power. So we read in Genesis about the very first con job. The enemy offers knowledge, which is power, but they already had both in their perfect relationship with the Father. It's easy to say, "Oh thanks, Adam and Eve, wow! How stupid could you be? " Until I look inside and see all the times that I have done the very same thing, trading the things of God for the things of man. I think we can all relate, but we'll get into that later.

So, like I said, things were going really well. Business was increasing every year, the kids were doing great with their lives, and we were at a time in ours where we could take a deep breath and live a little. The 4th of July was coming up, and we were preparing to enjoy our family and some close friends. It was too hot outside, as I said before, but we were going to celebrate anyway. However, on the evening of July 3 around seven o'clock my mobile phone rang and what I heard next was the most life altering sentence of my life. Olivia, a friend of our daughter Maggie, was screaming into the phone, "Mr. Faust, we've been in an accident. Maggie's been ejected and she's unconscious; she's breathing, I think." and then the call was dropped.

For some reason the volume on my phone was turned all the way up so my wife, seated next to me on the couch heard every horrifying word as I heard it. It was too late! There was nothing I could do to spare her those words. It wasn't just the words, but the terror in Olivia's voice. Since then I have come to know that we sometimes say a lot more with *how* we say something, rather than by what we actually say.

Michelle immediately screamed, "Oh God, please don't take my baby!" As she ran to the car, she was completely unaware that she had wet her pants in that moment of terror. My blood pressure immediately skyrocketed, and my eyes felt like they were being pushed out from the inside. If you are a parent, you need no further explanation of how we felt at the time. I know people say that we all process things differently, in different situations, but that's just not true when it comes to your children. I believe all parents feel the same way in those moments. If you do not have children, I can only offer a very feeble description. You feel helpless; literally gutted, ripped bare, mind raped and emotionally destroyed all in an instant. Every nerve, physical, mental and imagined is vibrating. And that's just the first few seconds. After that, it gets really bad. You find yourself on the battlefield of the mind, where the sound of the phone call plays over and over in quick, rapid succession drowning out the screams of your wife and even your own. When you think you can take no more, that it can't possibly get any worse, it does by a factor of at least ten. That's when you realize your imagination is running out of control, way out of control. Pictures of the scene of the accident, which you haven't even been to yet, begin to flash in and out of your mind in vivid HD color.

The accident was rated by the Texas Department of Public Safety as a zero to 1% accident on their rating scale. To put it another way, just reverse it. That's a 99 to 100% chance of certain death at the scene. It's just simple mathematics when you get down to it. Speed plus weight plus mass produces energy, a lot of energy. It's just a reality. Call it physics, science, whatever you want. But God evidently has His own kind of math. You see, in this place, $2 + 2 = 4$, that's just plain common sense, but with God $2+2$ equals $=$ "whatever He says" (period) and that also is just plain common sense.

Some of you are going to absolutely love this story and rejoice with us in it. Some of you are going to be challenged by a few of the details that you are going to read, and some of you are going to find it just too much, just too hard to believe. I will say that I have something in common with all of you. I too rejoice in it. I too am challenged by it. And I too have to remind myself sometimes of what I believe. The fact still remains. It is our story and by our, I mean all of ours, His children. It's a story about the power of God loose in our lives, and it's a story of His crazy love and His unbelievable mercy. In other ways, it's a story about His harsh response to my unbelief.

I am convinced that if you will open your heart and mind and ask Him to reveal His truth to you, it becomes clear that when we say "Nothing is impossible for God", something about that phrase just doesn't sound right. I mean it sounds good to say and I know it's in the word of God. But at this place in my life, it's just too small. It's not my intention to offend the original author, God Himself, nor the people He chose to write it. I just humbly offer they were wrong or at least their phrasing was. With what I have seen and what He has brought us through, I will forever 'reverse it' and say THE IMPOSSIBLE IS NOTHING FOR GOD! When we say nothing is impossible, it is like saying the common cold is not impossible, a broken arm is not impossible and EVEN cancer is not impossible. Do you see the escalation from something simple like a cold to something much more difficult like cancer, at least in our human perception? In contrast when we say the impossible is NOTHING, we have just given anything and everything in this life that could ever cross our paths a common denominator of being *nothing*.

My family now lives in a place of gratefulness that I never knew existed. I am a broken man "fixed". I have been humbled by His grace, broken by His love and freed by His mercy. We will never be the same. Thank God!

CHAPTER 2

When I Met God

Who is a God like you, who pardons sin and forgives the transgression of the remnant of his inheritance? You do not stay angry forever but delight to show mercy. You will again have compassion on us; you will tread our sins underfoot and hurl all our iniquities into the depths of the sea.
~Micah 7:18-19

To tell the story correctly, I will have to rewind a couple of decades or so. Don't worry, I'm not going to give you a play-by-play of the last thirty years. First of all, I don't think I have enough time or paper for that anyway. And as a side note to give all the real authors out there a good laugh, I am literally writing this with a standard size notebook and the very finest Paper-Mate gel fine point pen that Wal-Mart has to offer. I'm not too savvy or up to date on all the high-tech gadgets out there today, so I'm just going to hit the highlights, if you don't mind.

Speaking of highlights, one of the greatest happened to me when I was a junior in high school. In my estimation, I was pretty typical. At seventeen I was doing my own thing, getting grades that were acceptable to me, although weren't to my parents. Even though I was raised for the most part in a Christian home and was in church on most Sundays, youth group was definitely not my scene. The kids I knew who were at church every Sunday and then youth group later in the same week just seemed a little weird. I mean they just seemed out of balance. The proof of this was that they would bring their weirdness to school with them. Don't get me wrong, I didn't dislike them and they didn't dislike me, as far as I knew. Some of them were sort-of my friends. I had lots of all kinds of friends - rednecks, druggies, regular types, Christian kids, athletes and of course, I got along great with the intelligent types, too, but mostly out of necessity. I mean, how else was I going to pass algebra? I would live my life in balance. I said to myself, "A little of this, little of that." You know, spread things out, try to keep things level in this otherwise "out-of-plumb" world. Church was A-Okay with me, just like everything else was, as long as it didn't go overboard. I felt Jesus was a good man, the best even. And I had said the sinner's prayer a few times and even believed it "took", if you know what I mean. I just wasn't ready to get crazy about it.

Then one Sunday during the summer of 1983, everything changed. I don't remember what month, probably July because it was hot (my argument with the Lord about the Texas heat goes back a long time). I was seated on the back row and across the room from my parents, (it just wasn't cool to sit with your parents when you were about to be a senior in high school), I noticed the pastor had changed up the service. We were going to listen to him first and then finish with the music part at the end of the service. I didn't know which was stranger, that he had changed the service or the fact that I even noticed. Anyway, I found myself intently listening to him for some reason. Near the end of his "speech", which is what I would've called it at the time, he said something that I will never forget. He said that Jesus was anything but a good man. He was God or He was a crazy man, but you can't have it both ways. He said Jesus said things like, *I am the way, the truth and the life and no one comes to the Father but by me.* He's either God in the flesh or a lunatic but, He's most certainly *not* just a good man. I have absolutely no idea what he said next. But I remember feeling that I needed to make a decision. Something began to stir inside me that morning.

The music began to play and everyone stood up and began to sing, and singing turned to worship that day. Some began to raise their hands and others melted down, and in that moment I found myself reaching up to heaven. I felt so strange. Was I really reaching out in worship or were my hands above my head stretched toward the ceiling because other people's were? Was I a victim of some kind of mass hysteria? But I was able to leave them up or pull them down; my free will seemed to be working just fine. The song was over, the service had ended, and I was out the door.

Unbeknownst to me, God had plans for me. I

had no idea at the time the lengths He was willing to go to and had already gone to, the long suffering patience He would have to extend to me, and His many "set-ups" and ambushes that He would have for me. That's Christian-ese for divine appointments and prayer meetings. Life just wasn't the same after that. Had I heard too much? Was I now accountable? What was I doing with my hands in the air anyway? I soon noticed that trying to please everyone and 'fit in' to be acceptable to all the different types of people in my life just wasn't working anymore. It was not anything that I could put my finger on. I just didn't like me when I was doing the things I'd always done and being the person I had always been.

CHAPTER 3

God's Plans Far Exceeded My Own

*For I know the plans I have for you," declares the
LORD, "plans to prosper you and not to harm you,
plans to give you hope and a future.*
~Jeremiah 29:11

My senior year started, and it was back to the
structure of school. Maybe that's what I needed. But it
didn't seem to help; I began to notice things I had never
noticed before. None of the people I hung around with
seemed to be happy, except for one girl in my class,
Michelle Weaver. I had always known her to be an
outspoken Christian through high school and not bad
looking either. Words like unmovable, constant,
committed were words anyone who knew her would
readily use to describe her. But words like that don't
buy you a lot of friends during the immaturity of high
school. Don't get me wrong, she had her share of
friends, but they weren't near as diverse as mine. I
recognized later that it was by design. But something
amazing had happened to her during the summer
between our junior and senior years. I should probably

say, "she blossomed into a beautiful young lady". I said, *probably*, but I won't. She got hot. I mean, gorgeous. Girls were jealous of her, and guys were noticing her, myself included. She still didn't get invited to many parties though, being a Christian and all.

The school year drug slowly on like molasses in January (to use a Texas term, which means *really* slow). I'm sure it had something to do with algebra, but mostly I blamed it on a bad case of senior-itis and the fact that I couldn't accept I was discontent. My friends weren't as much fun as they once were, and neither was I for that matter. I couldn't shake the thought that God wanted something from me. Had I cracked the door and peeked inside, or had He opened it to me? Should I go in? Would He let me? Did I even want to? I knew one thing for sure, I needed to change some things. Late one night lying on my bed in the dark, I raised my hands to heaven. This time for real, and asked God to give me a friend, a true friend of His choosing. And then in that moment I realized I was a genius. I had heard somewhere when you pray, it helps if you're specific. You ladies don't know where I'm going with this yet, but the guys are already there. So I prayed, "Lord of all heaven and earth, I have but one humble request, please out of Thy great lovingkindness grant me but one blessing, a friend Lord, like Michelle Weaver." Okay, it wasn't quite like that, but my hands were in the air, that's got to account for something, right? I did mention her by name because she was the most real, committed Christian I knew. I guess I just wanted to help the Lord by providing a mental picture of my simple request. I had no clue about how to really pray. I mean sure, I knew how to pray over say... food, that's easy, you just say, "Lord, thank you for this food, bless it to the nourishment of our body, and bless the hands that prepared it." All I knew at the time was that God must really like that prayer because look how many times a day He gets to hear it! I was fairly well versed in Christian-ese but this was no time for that. This was important!

Over the next few weeks I began to notice that my inner radar antenna would be activated every time Michelle had an opinion or comment on just about anything. I noticed that she was liked by just about everyone and what's more, respected by staff and students alike. Even being voted Senior Class Vice President, and homecoming queen, she was true to herself and what she believed. Over time we got to know each other. It seemed like we would run into each other almost everywhere: in the library, study hall, lunch room, or in the hall after her volleyball games or practice. You know, all the usual places that I hung out... it was uncanny how much our paths crossed. I almost didn't notice at first because I was so focused on patiently waiting on God and studying. It is a wonder we hadn't missed each other.

That's my story. Now let me tell you His. Remember that strange experience I had in church, the summer Sunday on the back row with my hands in the air for what seemed like an eternity (but in reality was probably only a few seconds)? Michelle was there, and just happened to open her eyes long enough to get a quick glimpse of me from across the room. She was probably sitting near my parents. God uses anything and everything to bring about His plan, even my silly, immature seat choice that Sunday morning. He has a way of making me look way better than I really am. After all, every good father wants to make their son look good.

"For I know the plans I have for you declares the lord, plans of good and not of evil, plans to prosper you and not harm you, plans to give you a hope and a future." ~***Jeremiah 29:11***

He declared it; the Person who spoke the world into existence, is FOR me! It's now 2012 and Michelle and I just celebrated our 26th wedding anniversary. I asked for a friend and God just being Himself, gave me one of His choosing. Talk about pressed down, shaken together and running over!

CHAPTER 4

Life Has No Rewind Button

"See, LORD, how distressed I am! I am in torment within, and in my heart I am disturbed, for I have been most rebellious. Outside, the sword bereaves; inside, there is only death. ~**Lamentations 1:20**

I so wish I could avoid writing this chapter. I deeply regret many things in my past. I would love to candy coat it for you and whitewash it for my friends and many acquaintants that may read this book. If I could do things over again, I would. But life has no rewind button, does it?

It was the late 1980s. Texas was in the midst of an oil recession. Our economic outlook was bleak to say the least. Jobs were tough to find, good paying jobs even tougher. At the time, there was what some called the great Texan migration. Texans were leaving the state in droves to anywhere that had the promise of jobs. It was a stressful time in our state, our family was no exception. My wife had given birth to our first-born late one hot summer day in August, and I was feeling the heat of the responsibility of fatherhood. So I decided to try my hand at door-to-door sales. I was introduced to a very unique and simple product that I was convinced everyone needed. It was a little brown plastic box that mounted to the top of a door, designed to give a signal to alert business owners or employees that customers have just entered their business. It was a great product, inexpensive, made in the 'U.S.A', and had a five-year warranty. What's not to like, right? I was off and running in my new business venture, but all that glitters is not gold. It soon became apparent that to sell my wonderful little made in the U.S.A. device with its reinforced polymer plastics, no internal electronic parts, sleek design, free installation and a full, no questions asked five year limited warranty was not easy. You must first be at the right place at the right time, and this of course, is completely out of your control. Let me explain: in order to entice a potential buyer you must first find one. Finding businesses was easy. They were everywhere. But buyers with the authority to purchase my wonder product, well, that was an elusive creature, my friend. You see, most businesses don't give their managers the checkbook to make on the spot purchases. If you're lucky enough to catch the owner or manager with purchasing power present at the time you happen to walk into their business, well, you may have just struck gold.

Gold miners have a saying when standing on a fresh claim, "We're all rich with gold, boys, at this very moment. All we have to do is dig it up." You see, it's much easier said than done. Owner/manager types are typically an interesting species. They can smell a door-to-door salesman from a mile away, and they have the eyesight of an eagle. If they even sense your presence, they move in such speed out the back door or duck into the back room so fast, it's ninja-like. If you play your cards right you might corner one. This, I soon learned, took skill which, like gold-mining, was much easier said than done.

On an average day I would have to walk into at least 100 businesses, minimum, to increase my odds of catching my elusive prey. I found both early in the morning before the caffeine kicks in and late in the evening they seemed to move a little slower on their feet. Without boring you with much detail, some days I would sell five or ten units, some days one or two and on other days I got skunked. Zip. Zero. There's a saying in the sales industry, "Heroes are zeros at the beginning of every day." Meaning, no matter how well you did yesterday, today everyone starts at zero. That pat on the back you got yesterday quickly turns into a kick in the pants today. It's a "what have you done for me lately" thing. Most guys I knew in my line of work were working the map, striking out across the country searching for a better place to dig, hoping to find a good vein of sales and doing all they could to increase their odds. I was no exception.

Let me paint a quick picture for you. You tell your wife you're setting out in pursuit of the American dream, and it's all for the best, you'll only be gone a couple of days. Funny thing is, it doesn't seem like her American dream. So you pack up, load up and take off, telling yourself *a man's gotta do what a man's gotta do.*

Soon the overnight trips turn into a few days away from home. Then days turn into weeks.

Life on the road, seeing the country, meeting new people, no time clock, no stuffy office, what an adventure! *This is going to be great* you tell yourself. Then there's that pesky little thing called reality. As I drove down the road, off to points unknown, I painfully remember the look on her face as I pulled out of the driveway holding our daughter in her arms. Oh she tried her best to put on a happy face for me, but the look in her eyes gave her away.

There was one major part of the equation that I hadn't considered. When you enter over 100 businesses, minimum per day and you sell 0 to 10 units per day, it means you were told 'no' at least 90 times a day on your best day. I found out that my quarry had teeth and didn't mind using them on door-to-door salesman. To maximize profits, I had to look for ways to save on expenses, which can get out of hand on the road. I realized every dollar I spent, was a dollar I couldn't send home and that translated into more time on the road. Cheap motels on the seedy side of whatever town I happened to find myself in, and McDonald's drive-throughs were the norm. Even McDonald's became a luxury. It was less expensive to buy cheap lunch meat and day-old bread to make my own sandwiches.

Let me bring into focus an average day in my adventure on the road: Cheap backstreet motels, day old bread, and wilting lettuce floating in a Ziploc baggy in my ice chest. Oh, don't get me wrong. I would reward myself on successful days with a few beers just to celebrate, and you know, a few more when I wasn't so successful. As I slipped into the depressive blackness of my situation, beer turned to whiskey and my slipping turned to sliding. My daily dose of rejection and my nightly dose of whiskey began to take their toll. I'm not making excuses for my choices but in my experience, people don't like to blame themselves or take responsibility for their actions. More often than not we blame anything and everything or anyone, for that matter, but we rarely blame the man we see in the mirror, no matter how obvious his bloodshot eyes.

My self-esteem was in the toilet, partly because of the nature of my job, but mostly because of my view of myself. Still not able or wanting to blame myself, I began to blame Him. I mean, who else was there except God who put me in this horrible place? I knew He had the power to fix this entire nightmare, and I blamed Him when He didn't. One night in a drunken stupor I remembered what some religious nut had said: "All we have to do is stand on the Word of God and He will meet all of our needs." I reached into the nightstand for the Gideon Bible, but the handle of the cheap drawer came off in my hand. Enraged I thought, *I can't even get to the Word of God.* So I ripped off the whole front of the drawer, threw the Bible in the middle of the floor and stood on it, literally! Standing there, tears running down my face, I cursed Him. I told Him that He wasn't very good at His job either. *Where are You when I need You? And this Bible stuff is a bigger pile of baloney than my canned sales pitch.*

Upon waking the next morning in my usual hung-over, bloodshot fashion and feeling the weight of shame and self-hatred, I got my tools out of my truck and attempted to fix the nightstand so I wouldn't be charged for the damage. I headed for Texas, back to my wife and growing family.

I don't mean to make my experience on the road sound all bad, because I learned a tremendous amount about sales. It was like salesman Boot Camp. After hearing the word 'no!' several thousand times a month, you learn, that 'no' only means your prospective customer hasn't said 'yes' yet. So you figure out how to turn a 'no' into a 'yes', or you starve. I had more sales opportunities in a week's time than many salesmen have in a lifetime.

When I arrived home Hannah, our second daughter, didn't recognize me right away. Maybe it was because I tried to clean up my outward appearance a little before I got home by shaving off my beard. But I knew it was more than that. I just wasn't home enough for her to know me. I vowed at that moment that I would do whatever it took to stay home. I went through a short string of odd jobs, doing this and that to put food on the table. I also "worked late" a lot, which was code for drinking beer with my friends. None of this of course, escaped my wife. We maintained our relationship but had our share of arguments, which is putting it very mildly, mostly about my lifestyle. Life wasn't working.

CHAPTER 5

From Cheap Motels To A Suit And Tie

Lots of changes, but very little change...

In the early 1990s, my two brothers left the real estate business because of the poor economy. They started selling cars at a local dealership and were making a living. I thought to myself that there was no way selling cars could possibly be as hard as my previous sales experience. Working in the same town every day would be a treat. Heck, working in the same state would be a treat. No more crappy motels, no more soggy bologna sandwiches; I hate bologna to this day. It was sales, so I was prepared for some rejection, but it would be nowhere near the scale that I was used to. My older brother put in a good word for me and I got the job. The dealership carried brand-new cars with six different franchises and a good selection of used cars as well. Things were looking up and I felt much better about my prospects, almost to the point of being excited. Strangely, I remembered feeling the same way at the beginning of my last adventure. Little did I know I was about to go from the frying pan into the fire.

When I was hired it was because some poor guy got fired, leaving an empty desk. The office was all the way down a long hallway, the last door on the right. The only thing farther away from the sales action was the break room. So I spent most of my time roaming around the lot waiting for a customer. I quickly learned that this was what the average car salesman did, and I also noticed that the average salesman didn't make much money. I was getting bored with this strategy anyway, probably because my previous sales job was so intense. I was used to moving fast all day long, speaking to as many contacts as possible. It seemed nobody's job was safe, and the dealership went through almost as many managers as it did sales people. However, one of the old sales managers had a saying "hard work beats talent, when talent doesn't work hard." I thought it sounded more like something Vince Lombardi would've said. Maybe it was. But one day he said to me, "If you stick to the basics, you'll be fine."

The basics were easy: keep moving all day, work past sales leads that the dealership would provide if you asked, use the phone book to make cold calls, (which I hated 'cause it reminded me too much of door-to-door sales), send out thank-you cards, and ask everyone you know to refer people to you. The list goes on, but if you did the basics every day and you had some talent, you had a good chance to make a good living. As time went on, I got better at my job, partly because of the terrifying prospect of going back on the road and partly because I felt great about my newfound success. This was understandable because as I mentioned before, my self-esteem had taken a beating. I told myself that it was understandable given the situation I was in, being away from my young family, making just enough money to barely get by. A lot of other guys my age were somehow able to be with their wives and kids, and I was stuck. Do you see what was happening? I was still standing on that Gideon Bible in that cheap motel room, railing at God. The only difference was, now I was wearing a suit and tie, selling expensive cars instead of plastic doorbells. I was still me, no matter where I went.

CHAPTER 6

Checkmate

*Therefore, if anyone is in Christ, the new creation
has come: The old has gone, the new is here!*
~2 Corinthians 5:17

At this point I would like to introduce you to one of the weirdest people I have ever met in my whole life.

My two brothers had a friend. He would come to our dealership at least twice a week, sometimes more, to visit with one or both of them. He would talk about God every time he came and usually ended up praying for one of them. It freaked me out. It downright embarrassed me to watch it. Whenever I would see him drive in, I would get invisible, go to lunch, or just hide. A few times he trapped me in my office and wanted to talk about, you guessed it, God. My brothers eventually landed better paying jobs and were off to bigger and better things. But that didn't stop Richard. That was the weirdo's name, Richard Holcomb. Richard was a great salesman in his own right. He started out selling copy machines in the Houston area years ago and saved every penny he could. He risked it all to buy a small piece of ranch land near Kerrville, Texas. He turned around and sold it for profit and then did it again and again. When I met Richard he had bought and sold over one hundred thousand acres in the Texas Hill Country and was very well respected as a businessman.

As a matter of fact, during the worst economic time in Texas, his business thrived. When others were selling out, he was buying up, which was unheard of at the time. Wow! Talk about being at the right place at the right time. I thought, *what a lucky guy*. But if you ever asked Richard about it, get ready for a Bible study. He would immediately tell you it had very little to do with him and instead had everything to do with God's love, mercy and favor. Then he would usually start to tear up and try to pray for someone, *out loud* in a *car lot*, and in *broad daylight*!

This guy was a bonafide nut. But no matter what you thought of Richard, one thing was for sure. You knew he believed every word of what he said. Most liked him, but he just freaked me out, but that didn't stop Richard, and he became fixated on me. He would just show up at the car lot and want to visit. Visit! That's putting it mildly. Most of the time I could avoid him. Seemed that I'd learned a thing or two from all those "ninja-like" business owners and managers who used to try and avoid me. Richard would combat this the same way that I used to. He would just give himself more opportunities to catch me. Remember, I said he was a great salesman in his own right, and had many more years' experience, but I was fresh from Boot

Camp and knew a trick or two myself.

One day, one of our managers won a beer keg cooler in a raffle. To my surprise, upper management let him put it in the break room hidden inside a closet so if a customer happened to walk by and the door was left open, they wouldn't see it. Half the sales staff got off at 6 PM the other half at 8 PM. So the rules were: #1 you could drink beer as long as you stayed in the break room once you entered and didn't roam around with a beer in your hand, #2 when you left, quietly go out the back door, and #3 we had to pay for the beer. We thought about arguing rule #3, but decided not to push it and tempt fate. I thought this was very irresponsible of upper management, but at the same time I thought, *how awesome is this*. I had a keg cooler ten feet from my office, and not just any keg cooler. It was the 16 gallon variety, not just the backyard trash can style, either. This puppy was a stainless steel Freon powered commercial grade model. It wasn't long before someone brought a big screen TV and an old couch from a garage sale. Suddenly, the dealership decided to increase our hours of operation dramatically, or at least that's what we told our wives. In no time at, all the wide stainless steel top of the keg cooler became was a make-shift bar for you guessed it: whiskey. 'Round the mountain I went again. Being re-introduced to whiskey caused the level of my resistance to be almost nonexistent.

As my frequency with the booze increased, so did my visits from Richard. By this time I had been promoted three times to the title G.S.M., which stood for General Sales Manager. I had several sales people and three finance managers under my watch, and my income was approaching the six-figure range. I was given a brand-new Cadillac to drive and a retirement plan. I was even put on the company bar tab at the local resort-style hotel lounge so I could enjoy a more refined drunken experience. There was even talk of grooming me for my own dealership to operate as the General Manager.

Everything was escalating, my income, my position, my prospects, my drinking, fights with my wife and my visits from Richard. I had grown to accept Richard for who he was because I felt he accepted me for who I was. I had never hidden my lifestyle from Richard, partly because I had already tried to please everyone and that didn't work out too well. It was just exhausting, and mostly, I just didn't care. By this point in my life, I made what I thought was a complete recovery in the self-esteem department. I was a 100% different person. I had big bragging rights, a good income, a fancy car to drive, nice fat job title, and the power to hire and fire, all without the need for a higher education. Some people respected me, while others had to! To say the least, my ego was off the ego chart.

Then there was Richard. By this time we were well past all the small talk and hint dropping about God, and well into long talks that I would usually turn into arguments since my self-defense mechanism was to get combative when losing a conversation. I had some head knowledge about the Bible, way more than I had worked to earn myself. At a very early age my dad would put a cassette tape player in my room at night when I went to bed. He would play the Bible on cassette in my room all night, every night. I became almost addicted to it. I had to have it to sleep. This went on until junior high, when one of my friends noticed it in my room, and I became very embarrassed about it. I knew just enough to be dangerous with what I thought the gospel was. But with Richard I was outmatched. I wanted to argue points and topics by taking them out of context to serve my need at the time. Richard seemed to always take everything back to relationship and God's love. He was fond of saying, "In the real estate business the three most important things are location, location, location." He would say, "Troy, God is like that except it's relationship, relationship, relationship", to him God was about love, forgiveness, freedom and power. I never remember Richard mentioning religion or the Ten Commandments or hell's fire for that matter, either.

Richard would always invite me to church and I would always say no. "Been there done that," I would say or some other cocky statement. My wife was going to church almost all the time while I made excuses almost all the time. Oh, I would go on Easter for sure, because I was convinced that if you didn't, you went straight to hell. Do not pass go, do not collect $200.00. I also knew she was attending Bible studies. But what I didn't know was that they were the intense type. She was getting help and healing from a lot of things most, I'm sure, that I had had a hand in. She would receive sound counsel and receive prayer from some amazing women to whom I will always be eternally grateful.

They were there for her when I wasn't. In those times she would lift me in prayer and ask God to touch me and break my heart with how much He loves me.

On one occasion, not unlike a hundred before, Richard invited me to church. He told me about a special speaker, a close friend of his, who was coming to his church for a few days. I was starting to think that he had some kind of quota to meet. But for some reason I said yes. I have no idea why; I had perfected the art of saying no. He was genuinely excited, but I knew deep down that I had no intention of going. After all, it was just a slip of the tongue, I told myself. But what happened next almost defies description.

Monday morning, I was on the lot near the street thanking an elderly woman for her purchase. As she shut her door and drove away, I heard the horrible sound of screeching tires, and I turned around to see Richard's red Ford Bronco sliding to a stop, white smoke pouring out of all four tires. His door flew open and he came charging towards me, almost like he had been shot out of a cannon. The look on his face was one I hadn't seen before. He was mad and running straight at me. So I did the only thing I could think to do, I took off in the other direction! There I was, the suit wearing manager, running from this crazy mad man. I passed the parts department, the service department and around behind the body shop. I was almost 30 years younger than Richard, but I was amazed how quick he was that day. It might've had something to do with how hung over I probably was. I finally began to run out of air and got mad myself. I thought to myself, *I'm going to end this right here and now. I'm going to stop and turn around and cuss this Christian's whole family tree. When I'm done with him, he'll never ever come back here again.* Being a very seasoned salesman also meant I was a pretty good talker, and put together with my rough lifestyle, I could cuss the paint off of a wall. So I planted my right wingtip in the gravel, spun around, put my right finger in Richard's face and fully intended to let him have it. I mean, with both barrels, as they say.

Then it happened. I was frozen. I couldn't move a muscle; no words were coming out at all. By this point I should've been cussing a blue streak that would make a sailor blush, shaking my finger in his face, but nothing was working. It was like an angel had a grip on my tongue. I soon realized that Richard's finger was working just fine. He stuck it right in my face, gasping for air, and said, "You sir, are a liar and a coward." Then he slowly turned around, walked back to his vehicle and drove away. There I was, standing there in the dirt, sweating, looking at the back of my right index finger still stuck in the air. It was surreal, but there was more. As I was able to move a little I realized he was absolutely right. I was a liar and I was a coward. At the very least, I told him I would be at church on Sunday and I wasn't. I walked back to my office, slammed the door and sat down for a long moment trying to make sense of what had just happened. I didn't know how to feel. Was I mad, confused, convicted? I didn't know. The only way I know to describe it is that thoughts were racing through my mind slowly. I know that doesn't sound right, but it's as close as I can get. It was as if the photos of the scene snapped through my mind like an old-timey black and white slideshow, all the while Richard's words echoed in my head.

Before I knew it the phone was in my hand, and I was punching in my home number. Michelle answered with that voice that seemed to sound sweeter and more content each time she spoke. There was a reason for that, I found out much later; she had turned me over to the Lord. I was no longer her problem, I was His. Talk about being outmatched! She answered the phone, and I barked at her, "We're going to church tonight." No... hi, how are you, how's your day going. Just, "we're going to church." She replied with one word. "Okay", giving me no excuse to pick a fight or change the subject or my mind for that matter.

We showed up at the church a little early, I think by design. I'm pretty sure Michelle wanted to sit way down front for some reason. I was looking for my usual back row seat. You know, where you can see everything better and take it all in. She was having none of it, so she waltzed us right down to the second row, but at least I had a great aisle seat! There we were, all five of us, Michelle, pregnant with our unborn son, Megan, Hannah and me. This was the first time since Easter we were all together in church.

Before the service started, I saw Richard from across the room. When we made eye contact, I could see nothing I expected in his eyes. There was only kindness, compassion and a genuine gladness that I was there. Something began to stir in me, nothing big and moving, but more like a small pebble that had been dropped into the pool of my inner man. The music started and everyone in the small packed out church stood up. Immediately it seemed almost everyone in the room was in full worship mode. I'd seen something like this before. Those people were singing for all they were worth, some kneeling down, some looking very emotional. Boom! Just like that. There wasn't even any build up or warm-up. On second thought, I decided I hadn't seen anything like this before. Where was this going? The energy in that place was tangible, and I was getting nervous, almost scared. I felt at the very least, like a fish out of water. I thought, *if these people knew me, the real me, they would probably ask me to leave.* Half of me wanted to run out the back door, and fake an illness or something. But the other half felt like I was right where I needed to be.

Although it appeared everyone was worshiping, not everyone was. There were others there just like me. I prided myself on being an expert at reading body language, but come to think of it, I prided myself on quite a few things. However, it became obvious to me that I was right on this fact. There were others like me there, but the bigger question looming in my mind was, *how did they get here? Were there others like Richard running around town 'loose'?* It was obvious who they were, just standing there with their hands in their pockets or looking around, kind of like a deer caught in the headlights. I noticed that the words to the songs were being projected onto a large screen. So the choices were simple, sing-along and try to blend in or just stand there looking like a target for some holy roller zealot. I knew that your demeanor could attract one of them and cause them to feel led to come over and try to fix you. I was still reeling a bit from my experience earlier that day with Richard, so I decided to sing-along. After all, Richard and my wife were the only ones who knew I was really a complete fraud.

The truth was my wife had many people praying for me. However, she didn't go around uncovering my sin to just anyone who would listen. She only confided in a handful of mature Christian women (one of whom happened to be Richard's wife, Glenda) committed to stand believing with her for my very life. She defended me fiercely against all attacks, human or spiritual. But at this point she had in our relationship almost all she could take and was thinking about leaving me. After all, who would blame her, who could blame her? She was nearing the end of her rope, but I couldn't see it. My ego wouldn't let me. But instead she stayed, and she prayed. Wasn't that supposed to be my job? To protect her, to hold the line for what was good and right, to be there for her? For years I'd been on the road gone from my family, and even though my job had changed and I was home every night, I couldn't have felt further away from the people I loved the most.

So I began to sing, mostly for its camouflage effect, and there it was again. Something stirred in me like a waking creature. The pebble was working its sinister plan, rippling out in ever widening circles. Finally the music stopped, thank God. That's not to say I was thankful, I was just glad it was ending. A strange silence fell over the whole place. You could hear a pin drop. It seemed no one was even breathing, there was no moving around, no one sat down, no one headed off for a bathroom break. Nothing! Just pure silence. It was deafening. I sensed we were standing in front of the God we had just worshipped.

Richard went to the front of the room, picked up a microphone and started to introduce the speaker. Just so you know, I'm running pretty fast and loose with the word "introduce". That gives the connotation of someone standing up and saying some nice accolades and accomplishments of the person about to speak so the listeners have a little background. It's designed to make the experience more enjoyable. Instead, what really happened was that Richard raised the microphone to his mouth, but was unable to speak. The only thing that happened was that tears began streaming down his face when he would try to speak. *How embarrassing* I thought. I was used to this part of Richard's personality, I'd seen him cry before, but this was in front of a whole room full of people. Oddly enough, I felt protective of him. But I decided they obviously knew him around here. Maybe they were used to him too. Richard was finally able to get out a few very emotional words and sat down on the front row.

As Randy Clark took the stage and began to speak, I thought, *I can do this, it's almost over. All I have to do is just sit here. I should act like I'm listening intently. I mean, how many points would I score with the wife if she saw me in deep thought as Randy spoke? What about taking a few notes? Naw, that's overkill, she'd never buy it.* This was my plan, but God had a slightly different plan in store for me that night! Randy's sermon was about men being men, real men, godly men, the kind that lead their families in the ways of righteousness. He spoke about men that were in love with Jesus, who chose to put Him first in their lives. If a sermon was a suit, then this one was tailor-made for me. Uh oh! There it was again, that stirring deep inside, this time seasoned with a healthy portion of conviction.

I needed to focus, fast! So I pulled out my usual "make myself feel better" self-talk. I began telling myself things like, "You're not that bad. You're a good provider. You don't cheat on your wife like a lot of other guys. You're a good provider. You don't do drugs. You're a good provider." My list was ridiculous, especially in the light of that place, and I'm not referring to the fluorescent lights in the ceiling. I walked in feeling ten feet tall and bullet proof, by that point I was sure I could get out of building without ever touching the handle on the door; I could just slither under. *Was this ever going to end?* I thought to myself. Outwardly I looked pretty good. I was dressed in full Christian-ese camo, from the agreeable look on my face with whatever Randy said, to my attempt to join in with the sing-along thing. Fitting in had never been my problem, or at least projecting that illusion. Man, was this ever an illusion. Talk about hypocrite extraordinaire!

Richard was the only one there that knew who I really was, and he had invited me. My wife was another exception of course, and I assumed she didn't care; she was just happy I was there in the first place. As a matter fact, I assumed she was thrilled. After all, wasn't this what she wanted? There you have it folks, manipulation at its finest, but sadly I didn't even realize that the only one I was manipulating was the one sitting in my seat. At least I felt better; the service coming to a close, the finish line was in sight, and most importantly my wife would be happy with me. I even felt good for Richard, what with all the time and energy he had put into getting me here. All in all, the night was a success. Oh sure, I still had to deal with that little pebble thing, but I wasn't even sure if it had been real or imagined. I felt like I had done the right thing. Even back then I knew you had to give a little back from time to time.

Randy was having a hard time ending the service. He had already brought it to a close once or twice, and then to my disbelief, he asked the band to come back. I thought to myself, *This guy is never going to make it in this business.* Even I knew how a church service was supposed to go. You have some announcements, then you pass the plate, then you have some music, then the pastor speaks, then you pass the plate again. It wasn't that complicated.

Randy said he felt like the Lord wanted him to pray for some men there that night, to pray a father's blessing over them. He wanted to lay hands on them and ask the Lord to give them power and freedom in their lives to be the men and fathers the Lord had called them to be. Almost immediately, several men went down to the front and formed a half circle with Randy in the middle. People began to move the chairs that were on the front row to make more room, which meant, I was now on the front row.

Wow! Talk about so close, yet so far away! The first guy in line to be prayed for was oddly enough a guy I had seen before, many times actually. He was a regular at the hotel lounge down the street from the dealership. We had only spoken once or twice. He was a plumber, big guy, lots of tattoos, a few years older than me, I guessed. I didn't know him but I definitely didn't like him. It wasn't anything I could put my finger on, but he just seemed like a tough guy, kinda cocky. Every time there was a football game on the TV above the bar, he would always have a comment, usually a loud comment or some statistical observation about whatever team was playing. That's about all I remembered, except that I didn't like him.

The band played softly and it seemed like everyone was being very quiet and reverent. Some were making their way toward the door while most sat and seemed to be praying. Something occurred to me at that moment. I hadn't checked to see how the kids were doing with all this stuff going on. So I looked down where my daughters were supposed to be and they were not there. Their seats were empty. Where were my daughters? A very familiar feeling of fear gripped me. A stinging feeling started at the top my head, my face began to flush, and sweat began to form on my forehead. My heart racing, I was propelled into kill mode. I mean that quite literally. Gripping Michelle's arm probably too hard, I started to ask, but before the words could clear my mouth, she knew what the look on my face meant. She looked into my eyes and said,

"They are in kid's church. And yes, I am positive." She knew me and she knew that a cursory answer would not do.

Let me try to explain. Over the last few years, basically since our children had been born, I had become very overprotective of our children, or at least that's what everyone said. I thought to myself, *they're crazy! How is that even possible? How can you be overprotective of your children?* But I knew that I was not right because being right wouldn't feel like I felt. Of course I had never talked about it with anyone else, not even Michelle, mostly because I didn't think I had a problem. No matter what she thought, I was being a good father. If a man won't protect his own children, then he didn't deserve to live. If it sounds harsh and irrational, even a little, then congratulations, you have just scratched the surface of the Mount Everest of my craziness when it came to my kids. Proud of myself for being an excellent protector, there was *no way* anything was going to happen to my children on my watch, period. I would rather die. Correction, I would have loved to die in the act of protecting them. I could think of no better way! I needed to see them with my own eyes to really believe that they were O.K. My fear had absolutely nothing to do with Michelle's mothering abilities, because in my opinion, she was a perfect mother. It had everything to do with my psychotic problem. I trusted Michelle and her alone when it came to the kids. This was one place in our marriage that we were of the same mind, except that her mind was healthy.

The service was almost over and I would believe Michelle's assessment that the kids were all right, but my mental clock was ticking. Soon I would have to see them with my own eyes. My mania about the kids had interrupted my thoughts about the service. My mind refocused.

Randy walked up to the first guy, the tattooed plumber, and simply laid his hand on his shoulder. He leaned in and whispered something into his ear. The whole thing took maybe ten or twenty seconds and then the tatted-up tough guy fell face forward to his knees and began to weep. I don't mean cry, I mean, broken, weeping, ugly crying! I thought, *how embarrassing. I can't believe he's freaking out like this! I mean, damn man, really, get hold of yourself!! I understand it's tough, but really!* The picture in my head was, *we're all in this thing together, tough guy! And you couldn't even make it to the backdoor!* I also couldn't believe how excited and genuinely happy I was because there was no way I was going to let this tough guy live this down. OH! I was going to make sure that we got to know each other now! I couldn't wait to drop a hint later that I was there that night, and then watch him crawl. Let's see how Big Mouth feels after I'm done with him! I was always looking for a fight, physical or mental. I was rotten. Here's proof for all you Christians out there that think I was just a hurting young man, lashing out. The truth is, I wanted to embarrass him, I wanted to hurt him, push whatever button I had to, to get a reaction. His ugly crying scene on the floor of that little church that night was just too much ammo, too juicy, how could I not use it? Why not? Why did I want him or need him to hurt? I didn't even know him!

Then, as I was standing there on what used to be the second row, somebody bumped me on my left side, and I turned to look. A guy was standing beside me looking straight ahead, tears already forming in his eyes. I turned toward Michelle, but she was gone, and in her place was another guy. A second row of men was forming, and I was right in the middle of it. Crap! How could I let this happen? Where was Michelle? I had been lost in my imagination, planning the plumber's demise. Now look at me! Only moments ago I was sitting on the second row blending in, now I was standing in the second line of guys, directly below one of the recessed spotlights in the ceiling. So I just stood there, like a deer caught in the headlights. Bolting for the door came to mind. Was this some kind of a cosmic chess game? If so, I was losing.

Randy started down my row and I said a prayer, not out loud but in the privacy of my mind. I didn't know how long had it been since I had directed words toward God. I'm not sure it was so much of a prayer as a statement or demand. I will never forget it is long as I live and it went exactly like this, "God, I want two things: #1 if You touch me, I want to know it's You, not me being over-emotional like the idiot bawling on the floor, and #2 I want You to grow me up fast." An odd thing to say I know, but that's exactly what I said. In hind sight, it was an extremely arrogant prayer. I had the audacity to stand there and make demands of God Almighty. If I were Him I would've zapped me off the planet.

Batter up! It was my turn. Randy was standing in front of me looking me right in the eye. I chose to keep my eyes open, unlike the other guys in line. I dug in, stiffened my spine and stood there, defiant as a rock. I wasn't going down, and I sure wasn't going to get all gooey. Randy put his right hand on my left shoulder and just looked at me. No words came out; he just stood there looking at me. *What in the world is going on now,* I thought. He closed his eyes, and I thought, *O.K. Here it comes, he's summoning up a little extra power. After all I'm a pretty tough nut to crack.* I was sure the look on my face had given me away, and I knew I had on the wrong camo for this situation.

Then the unthinkable happened. He opened his eyes and looked at me, eyes full of compassion and at the same time a little confusion, and stepped over to the next guy in line. Oh he wanted to pray for me, but he just couldn't. Why? It was like he didn't have permission or something. What in the hell was going on? I couldn't even get prayed for! Then it hit me, I had made God mad. Wow, I knew I wasn't the sharpest tool in the shed, but this was a new level of stupid. The God of the universe! We're talking God Almighty here. It was true that I didn't want to join His club and play some kind of a plastic Jesus game, but this was just dumb. Did I really have to poke Him with my silly little demands? Thoughts like, *How am I going to get Michelle and the kids home began to creep in my head.* I was sure that I was going to die in a fiery car wreck or something because I made Him mad. I knew He wouldn't hurt my kids though. As a matter of fact, the only time I could manage a prayer was when it concerned the kids. Still, I was in big trouble!

I had to take action, I had to do something. Just standing there wouldn't do. So I slowly backed up and made my way down to the end of the line and tried my very best to look like someone else. Camo, that's what I needed, and not just any camo, I mean the good stuff. So I assumed the position, bowed my head and lifted my hands up out in front of me, palms up. You know, "when in Rome, do as the Romans do". I thought, *This is going to work.* Who in their right mind wouldn't pray for someone that looks like this? Just like before, Randy stood right in front of me, and just like before he put his hand on my shoulder, and just like before, nothing, just that same look on his face. Then he was gone.

The hair on the back of my neck stood straight up and fear made itself comfortable. This was getting serious now. I had given it my best shot, played my best cards, but to no avail. The music was coming to an end, and then I saw her. A little old lady was eye-balling me from across the room and she made a beeline through the crowd, headed right for me. Oh crap! This was the last thing I needed. Then I realized that I was naked, no more camo, just a big fat target on my forehead. I was sure she would mean well, but the last thing I needed was a local trying to fix me. What I needed was Randy, the hired gun to get back over here and untie the knot in my soul.

As a last ditch effort I assumed the position of deep meditation, eyes closed, palms up. I mean, who would bother someone when they're in deep thought, having a private moment with their Maker? I would wait her out. I was in no way prepared for what happened next. The second she got to me, she took her knobby little finger and poked the middle of my chest, hard, I might add. Shocked, my eyes snapped open, and I stared down at this frail little old lady. Little did I know she was anything but frail. She said in a fairly loud and extremely powerful voice, "God's got a word for you, do you want it or not?" Let me pause for a moment to remind you that I said there were going to be some very challenging things written in this book. This is one of them. I guess the look on my very perplexed face said, "yes." She looked me squarely in the eyes and said, "WHEN I TOUCH YOU, YOU WILL KNOW THAT IT IS ME AND I WILL GROW YOU UP FAST." She repeated the same exact words of my arrogant prayer verbatim, "Checkmate!"

Would you like to know what I looked like in that moment? Let's just say I had something in common with the plumber. I looked just like he had. I fell to my knees in a split second. Broken, weeping, snot pouring out my nose. Ugly crying doesn't even begin to describe what I looked like. The lady on the other end of the knobby little finger was named Latriece Harper, and I had a sense that she was just getting started. I didn't know it at the time, but she was the leader of the pack of prayer warriors that my wife had been meeting with. With her hand on the middle of my back she prayed for me, and when I say that she prayed for me, I mean she *really* prayed for me. It didn't sound anything like my meal time prayer I would say with the kids at dinner time. If I could cuss the paint off a wall, Latriece could pray the paint off a wall. Make no mistake, God hears all of our prayers, no matter our level of immaturity or maturity, but that doesn't change the fact I would come to appreciate that she knew what she was doing. She spoke to some of the roots of my issues and proclaimed things and called into existence things that were not as though they were (Romans 4:17b). It was in these moments that I knew that He knew me, the *real* me and loved me anyway. I sensed that others had gathered around my writhing body and began to intercede for me. Through my tears I caught a glimpse of someone else on the floor next to me; it was Richard. He was lying on the floor next me, praying for me and weeping almost as hard as I was. He grabbed me and held me in his arms as I wept. I clung to him for all I was worth. I wanted to die, so I did; and God raised me up off of that floor a new creation in Christ.

I have tried to explain what had happened to me that night many times. But mere words cannot express what God did in me and for me. My best attempt would be this analogy. If you took all of the information in all of the computers inside the Pentagon, and put it into your small little computer at home, your PC just couldn't handle it. Overloaded, it would crash like I did. It's just too much information. As I wept I could envision myself standing on that Gideon Bible. I knew that He had seen me too, and loved me anyway. Then another wave of emotion swept over me, almost growling through clinched teeth, in pain and tears at how I must have hurt Him. I realized this was a "divine set-up". I was ambushed by His unreasonable love, His merciful plan to break my heart wide open in an instant. He was the Warrior King, coming to save me from the prison I had built for myself. I began to see scenes in my mind where I had hurt Michelle deeply, and I was so ashamed. However, I quickly found out that God doesn't deal in shame. It's the enemy who deals the cards of shame to anyone who will receive them. I began to confess my sins to Him and immediately felt them lose their grip on my life. I didn't feel so tough now! Webster's Dictionary: tough: strong or firm but flexible, not brittle; not easily broken; characterized by severity or uncompromising determination; capable of enduring strain, and hardship. By definition I wasn't tough at all; in fact I was pretty weak and brittle, certainly not very flexible and definitely marked by compromise. But also by definition, I realized God was tough!

To this day I love praying and ministering to tough people or those who think they are. It's the gooey ones that I have a problem with, the people who say they believe in a higher power but can't tell you His name. But that's another story.

Latriece became my spiritual grandmother and stood in faith with Michelle and me for many years. I affectionately gave her the nickname, 'Thunder Finger'! She is with the Lord now, but I am convinced she still prays for me! Richard and Glenda became my spiritual parents and our closest friends on earth. Richard is and has always been there for me, on my best days and on my worst. We hunt and fish together and serve together at our church. I love him. It has been a great privilege to call him my friend these many years and greater still that he calls me one.

CHAPTER 7

The Holy Spirit Makes A Mess

You have to break a few eggs if you are going to make an omelet.

The next day I realized that everything was different somehow. I had been touched in my inner man and had become completely whole. I felt light and free, ready and willing to do the work of the service. That, my friend, is *complete* B. S., and I don't mean Bible Study. It would've been awesome if that's how it worked, but I was still me the next morning when I awoke. Don't get me wrong, God had most definitely touched my inner man. He had done so much in me and for me that I just couldn't explain it using something as inept as language. It would be wonderful to be able to describe the scene of my inner man that way. I would love to tell you that the sun was shining, birds were chirping, and that I could hear angels singing.

But the truth is that the scene looked more like a battle field in total destruction, like a bomb had gone off with buildings toppled over everywhere, some burnt, some still burning. There was the smell of smoke in the air and the streets of my mind were filled with rubble from the blast the night before. Preconceived ideas about God, bricks of fear and pain, lies, deceit, plans and traps that the enemy had set for me that I hadn't even noticed before, all lay on the ground everywhere. The Prince of Peace had come into the camp I had built, and He destroyed it with His unreasonable love and ridiculous mercy.

My heart was a mess of gargantuan proportion and the cleanup looked insurmountable, and it would have been if the Lord hadn't built relationships with Richard and Latriece and a few others along the way. Thank God these people didn't see me as a trophy on their shelf of spiritual accomplishments, but instead were more than willing to roll up their sleeves and get to the dirty work of discipleship. The cleanup would take awhile, then foundations laid and then the building process.

I was in church almost every time the doors were opened, and bought every book that was recommended to me. I listened to taped sermons that Richard would give me and he had quite a collection, which didn't surprise me. He even asked me to help him lead several men's Bible studies. Me! I said that he was a kind, patient and loving man; I didn't say he was smart. Humor aside, it was all part of discipleship training for me. He would tell me things at the time that just didn't make sense, like, "you get more of what you give away". He called it the economy of God. I trusted Richard completely and why not, look at what he had allowed the Lord to do through him. He was in agreement with the Lord concerning me, and had laid down his life for me. It had cost him something, his time and energy, to say the least, and I required a lot of both.

I quickly realized just because I had an experience with God didn't mean the fight was over. As a matter of fact, it meant that new war fronts had opened up with new tricks I had never seen before. It felt like the enemy had a play book for whatever situation arose. Does that sound familiar? There you are, in church all the time and everyone is so proud of you. You're leading Bible studies by yourself now, giving away what you have been given and seeing others healed in much the same way that you were. You might even be asked to preach in area churches and give your testimony. You help in kid's church, lead a home group and you even stop being a cowardly thief... you know, you start tithing. Ouch! Sorry...

So there you are learning to swing your sword, kickin' some devil butt, because after all you represent the King! And then you fall, hard! It seems you begin to repeat those old familiar sins more often, or at least you feel tempted to the point of entertaining those thoughts. The question is, what are you going to do about it? Unfortunately, many of us fall victim to this temptation because we can't ask for help or admit failure, especially if we have a job at the church. What will my wife or husband think? Or maybe you even hold some titled position! What will the church leaders or the pastor think? Let me repeat the question. It's simple, but let me repeat it anyway. What are you going to do about it? Many of us say, "It's a mistake, I won't do it again." We seem to say this over and over again. Sometimes, over time this method even works. The process of trial and error, which is just code for "getting sick of it", while we mature a little, works together with those sovereign acts of God's freeing power.

But there is a better, faster and more thorough treatment for the harsh destructive plans that the enemy has for us. I won't say that it's painless because it isn't.

*"Confess your sins one to another so that you may be healed, the prayer of a righteous person is powerful and effective." ~**James 5:16***

The enemy isn't kidding when it comes to his evil plan for you. He bets on the fact that some of us are going avoid pain and embarrassment at all costs. He double downs on his bet because unfortunately, he's seen it work time after time, keeping us in bondage and our relationships with God and man superficial. If we will learn the benefit of being brutal with ourselves, shining the light of truth and freedom on our sin, then we will strike fear in the mind of the enemy. Where then is he to hide? Remember he loves the shadows of our lives. It is a part of renewing your mind, Romans 12:2. Here's one fun way to look at it, you can renew your mind, but he can't. That's why he's in a constant state of depression. Here's proof, just think about the differences between your future and his.

CHAPTER 8

Tale of Two Houses

*I have no greater joy than to hear that my children
are walking in the truth.* ~**3 John 1:4**

One day as I was talking to the Lord in prayer, a
sense of thankfulness began to rise up in me. I began to
thank Him for just about everything I could think of.
Near the end of my prayer I began to thank Him for all
of the men He had brought into my life to mentor and
disciple me. As I prayed, the differences between those
men and me became obvious. I mean, you could almost
see halos on their heads if the light was just right. They
just shone with His presence; you just knew they
followed Him. At that moment a picture of a two story
house popped into my head. It was a vivid picture. It
was a pretty average looking house, except every
window had a bright light shining out of it, even the
little window in the front door where you would look to
see who was there if someone were knocking on the
front door. I said, "What's that?" He said "That's them."
I replied, "Yep, that looks like them all right."

Then another picture of a house popped into my

head. It was the same type of house, but the only light coming out came from the little window in the front door. So I asked, "What's that Lord?" And He replied, "That's you." I replied, "Yep, that looks about right." He said, "Son, I knocked on the door of your heart and you opened the door to Me and I came into you and made you Mine. Then you made Me as comfortable as you could in the entryway of your life." It became obvious, those men had invited him into every area of their lives which was why light was shining from every area of their lives and the Lord said, "Yep, that's right." That day I began to invite the Lord into other areas of my life, beyond the entryway. Some of the rooms I was proud of and some I didn't even want to go into myself. Others I had nailed shut with a thousand nails and didn't think I would be able to open, even if I wanted to. He was so kind to me when I denied Him access and said, "When you're ready we'll go in together." A friend of mine says that the Lord is the kindest person he has ever met. I agree!

While I'm on the subject of trusting God, don't freak out, but I'm going to touch your money in the next few sentences and then I promise, no more money talk. I phrase it that way, "I'm going to touch your money", to provoke your protective instincts, to help you let what you're about to read sink in. Benjamin Franklin was known for many things, one of which was his very creative quips. Most of you have probably heard this one before. "Beer is proof enough that God loves man and wants him to be happy." Okay, that one doesn't really fit, I just like it. The next one isn't as well known, but it sure does fit this topic. Ben said, "In my experience, the last place a man is converted is his purse." Let's say one night you're sitting in your Lazy Boy watching Monday night football or whatever, and you hear a knock on the door. You open the door and there stands Bill Gates. He informs you that you have won the grand prize in a drawing you didn't even know that you were entered in. What luck! "What did we win? What did we win?", you say with great excitement. Bill tells you that he is going to manage your money for life!! What would you do? I'll tell you what you would do. You would go out and get three more jobs so you would have even more money for him to manage. After all, this guy knows something about makin' money, right?

Sadly, some of us still think that God doesn't know as much about money makin' as Bill. That's just the trust side of things; the fact is, it's not really your money in the first place. I dare you to REALLY read this next scripture with an open mind and a heart willing to receive the truth.

"Will a mere mortal rob God? Yet you rob me. But you ask, How are we robbing you? In tithes and offerings. You are under a curse, your whole nation because you are robbing me. Bring the whole tithe into the storehouse, that there may be food in my house. Test me in this, says the Lord Almighty, and see if I will not throw open the floodgates of heaven and pour out so much blessing that there will not be room enough to store it. I will prevent pests from

*devouring your crops, and the vines in your fields
will not drop their fruit before it is ripe, says the
Lord Almighty. Then all the nations will call you
blessed, for yours will be a delightful land, says the
Lord almighty." ~Malachi 3:8-12*

People, it's time to *believe* God and not just *in* Him. I'm
not just feeding you a line here. I have struggled with
this stuff too, in the past. But I have come to believe it's
much better to confess my sin than to hold on to it,
wasting time and energy worrying about what someone
is going to think instead of what God thinks. After what
I have seen God do with that opening of the heavens
thing, it has now become a pleasure to tithe, not a
chore.

Most of our financial problems are in fact, trust
problems. Michelle and I have had the pleasure of
ministering to a lot of marriages over the years, and I
can tell you for a fact that a huge percentage of
arguments in marriages are about money. To say it
another way, many fights could be easily avoided if we
would commit to trusting the Lord with our/His money.
Money has something in common with sex in marriage.
When it's good, you hardly talk about it. When it's not
so good, it's all you seem to talk about. You know, it's
like putting our money where our faith is. Okay, I'm
almost done. Let me make a suggestion here, don't let
the enemy beat you up about it, and don't beat yourself
up either. Just talk to Jesus and ask Him to help you
trust Him! He loves that, by the way. I know it sounds
too simple. If it helps, just remember that the Bible calls

us sheep, and sheep are stupid. So He's got to help us, right?

The last few paragraphs have been on two totally different fronts. But they have a common denominator; they both are places that we are all confronted, either by the enemy or our own ingrained independence. They affect us all, in the deep places of our humanity. We say, "It's my private life and nobody's business." After all, we all make mistakes, or it's my money, I earned it. Or some other bla, bla, bla, nonsense excuse! I say it's a nonsense excuse because we were bought with a price and He has given us all a blood-bought right to be in intimate relationship with Him. He bled all over our sin and by not trusting Him with something as temporal as money, it's just stupid. It's not my opinion, it's His. He understands His provision for you is an ocean and He wants us to come to that understanding. Please know I am most definitely talking about your money, because it's a great example that we can all associate with. But that's the least of what this is about. Here's a Richard-ism for ya, "If you let God put His hand in your pocket, then you get to put your hand in His pocket." That is true no matter the subject; your time, your treasure or your talent.

Do you realize how much ground you would possess and freedom you would enjoy if you would eliminate these battlegrounds by applying these simple truths to your life? You see, it's about trust and falling in love with the King, but the enemy wants to make it about a fight. Here's my humble advice, give up and just trust Him and in doing so, you not only rob the enemy of the joy of seeing you struggle, you give the Lord His greatest joy of seeing you walk in His truth. Remember His words in 3 John 1.

"I have no greater joy than to see that my children are walking in the truth." ~3 John 1:4

But sadly Hosea says:

"MY people perish for lack of knowledge." (emphasis mine) ~Hosea 4:6

But here's the deal, we get to choose.

Much like the twelve spies described in the book of Numbers, Joshua and Caleb believed, and the ten lost their faith and then their lives. Their words revealed their true thoughts and condition of their hearts in one of the greatest slips of the tongue in history. Numbers, and there it is, right there in the middle of the sentence,

"We were grasshoppers in our OWN sight." ~Numbers 13:31

Their words had cursed them and affected all of the children of Israel. They all knew the same truths, that wasn't their problem, applying it was. Now let's compare their actions to this young teenager named David when Israel was confronted by a giant problem named Goliath. There in 1 Samuel check out the second sentence,

"David ran quickly toward the battle line to meet

him." ~1 Samuel 17:48

You know the rest of the story. We are still talking about David, Joshua and Caleb a zillion years later, and we don't know the names of the cowards. Cowards, that's a little harsh, so let me "church speak" it up for you: "They were just in a season of their lives where they weren't at a place to commit to the depths of what God wanted for them". This of course, is not the pesky truth of what we find in the Word of God. Instead, He led them back out into the desert until they died, then He gave their kids a shot.

I mention these areas because they were some of the first places God began to work in me to keep His promise to grow me up fast. I mention these two stories because, like them, we will all get our chance to rise up with courage or shrink back in fear.

CHAPTER 9

When Believing In God Is Not Enough

Then you will know the truth, and the truth will set you free. ~**John 8:32**

We just talked about the children of Israel concerning their first attempt to enter the Promised Land. Now let's rewind a bit and take a look at the Lord's heart for them when He led them out of Egypt in Deuteronomy 6:11. A friend of mine taught me what the Lord had shown him about this scripture. He said to think about the blessing that the Lord had promised them. The Lord said that He was going to give them houses that they hadn't built, wells they didn't dig and vineyards they didn't plant. Now filter it through their previous experience of being in bondage and slavery for 400 years. Not getting beaten would have been a great blessing, having enough food to eat would've been a great blessing and not seeing their children's ribs for lack of nutrition would've been considered a great blessing. So the magnitude of the Lord's promise and intentions for them must have been more than they could ever imagine. But that doesn't change the Lord's intent, does it?

What promises and intentions does the Lord have for you, I wonder, and will you choose to believe Him? Sometimes believing isn't enough. The Lord wants to teach us about agreement. The ten spies believed that the land across the Jordan was the promised land. But only Joshua and Caleb agreed with the Lord that He would bring it about. Believing is knowing that the *Lord can do it*. Agreeing is saying that the *Lord will do it*. I'm not talking about a "blab it and grab" theology. For me, it's very similar to John 8.

*"Then you will know the truth, and the truth will set you free." ~**John 8:32***

When I came to a saving knowledge of Jesus Christ and confessed my sins and asked Him to come into my heart and not only be my Savior but also my Lord, He did. In that moment He wrote my name on His own heart and commissioned an angel to write my name in the Lamb's Book of Life. I had just experienced the most important event I would ever have with the Lord. So I knew the truth and it set me free. Thank you, Lord. But it's also just as true to say in practical application that in the process of life, just knowing the truth will not set you free.

Think of it this way. Let's say that you have a deep cut on your left arm and you are rushing to the emergency room. The doctor comes to you with a large bandage with a blood clotting agent and he puts it in your right hand and tells you to put it on the cut and apply pressure. He leaves to get the sutures to sew up your arm, but while he's gone you just sit there bleeding never applying the bandage. The sad fact is, you are going to bleed to death with the cure in your hand. The truth will not set you free until you apply it. Truth is a wonderful event when it comes to salvation, but we must agree with the Lord and apply His truth in the process of our lives. I think that we can all agree life has a lot more process than it does big events. For a long time I thought that scripture was only talking about salvation but as so many things with God, there's another meaning as well. Any way you look at it, we need to know Him in the event and in the process of life. It's about believing in God and the importance of also believing God.

This reminds me of one Sunday during praise and worship that in my spirit the Lord said, "Troy it's not good enough to believe in me anymore." Of course at the time I wasn't sure if it was the Lord speaking because it just didn't sound right. I mean, of course believing in God is enough. Heck, it's more than enough! I was on the verge of rebuking some evil spirit trying to confuse my mind and pull me away from the Lord, when I heard the words, "Oh stop it, you know My voice, why don't You ask me what I mean?" To that I responded, "Yes sir." He began to reveal to my heart and mind that I had experienced an event with Him when I was saved, but that life is more about process than events. Salvation is believing in Him, but what was I going to do with the rest of my life? I needed to start believing Him. I soon realized that believing God is very different from believing in God. Just as the grave, the empty grave, is different from the cross. Sometimes we get stuck at the cross, and we forget about that empty grave. This became apparent to me one day when again, during praise and worship we were about to have communion, and I told the Lord that I just didn't dig communion. It just seemed ritualistic to me, somehow.

Of course I knew I was wrong, and He wasn't because He said in the Word, do this in remembrance of Me. Feeling a little guilty about my not liking communion, I didn't press the issue. But a few minutes later He did. "Thank God" because it was one of the biggest lessons I've ever learned within the span of just a few seconds. Now I love communion. He told me, "Troy, this is what I want you to do. Do specifically this and say specifically that. These are specific instructions. When you put the cracker in your mouth only say these specific words, "Thank you for dying for me." When you put the grape juice in your mouth say, "Thank you for living for me." At that moment I understood the difference between the cross and the grave. I guess I had already basically known the difference, but now I knew it in a way that caused me to agree with it. So there I stood, tears rolling down my face with the knowledge that He didn't just die for me, He is just as intent on living for me. He used the word specifically a lot in that lesson. When I reflected on it later that day, He was saying, even showing me, how specific the job of the cross was and also how specific the job of the empty grave was. He didn't just come to die for us, He also lives for us. He died for freedom's sake, your freedom, not only from things, but into things as well.

The Bible tells us that we have a high priest that intercedes for us daily. Simply put, it means Jesus is praying for you every day. The question is not if He's praying, but what's He's praying. He wants us to learn to agree with Him. Before this, I knew Jeremiah 29:11.

"I know the plans I have for you, plans for good and not for evil, plans to give you a hope and a future."
~Jeremiah 29:11

But here's the problem, I only believed it for you or someone I assumed had it all altogether, but I had a hard time believing it for me. But not anymore. I have ownership of Jeremiah 29:11. God says it's mine. However, He's always said that. The difference now is I believe Him. The enemy wants me to think I'm being arrogant or presumptuous, but I didn't put those words in the Bible. Those are God's words, and He wants me to believe and apply them to my life. It's His idea. Who am I to monkey with His idea?

Now, when I come across these amazing scriptures, I stop rationalizing why they're not mine and start enjoying the fact that they are mine. Just for fun, you want to talk about something that sounds really arrogant? The Lord told me one day that I am His favorite and made me go into my bathroom and look at myself in the mirror and say to myself until I was convinced. After a long while I stopped, knowing it was a fact that His love for me is so deep that somehow using the word favorite was too small. See what He does? He takes us from being apprehensive and a little embarrassed about saying "I'm His favorite", to understanding that in the depth of His love, the word favorite is just too small. We are three-dimensional. He might be 27 million dimensional, I don't know, but I do know we can all be His favorite. You know what's coming next: put down this book and go find a mirror! Try it, you'll like it! If for no other reason than the devil hates it.

CHAPTER 10

The Battlefield Is NOT The Soul

The weapons we fight with are not the weapons of the world. On the contrary, they have divine power to demolish strongholds. We demolish arguments and every pretension that sets itself up against the knowledge of God, and we take captive every thought to make it obedient to Christ.
~2 Corinthians 10:4-5

I was running late for work one morning, when I walked past my Bible that had been catching dust lately, and decided to play a little Bible roulette. You know, you've done it too. But for all of you out there that won't admit it, it goes like this. Grab the Bible and quickly open it at random, and throw your finger down and read what great wisdom the Lord has for you that day. Okay, it's not the best study tool, and I don't recommend it. But remember the Lord can use whatever He wants to teach His kids. The funny thing about God is, He thinks He's God, and He usually doesn't ask my permission to be Himself.

So there I was with my finger on some scripture

that was explaining how the battle is for the mind. I read a little and jumped in the shower. Standing there in the shower, it hit me. That can't be right because the battle is for the soul, right? I mean, that's what Jesus died for, right, the soul of man? That's the only thing we're getting out of here with our soul. I was convinced I had found a typing error in my Bible. Wow! What's the chance of that? As soon as I was out of the shower I picked up my wife's Bible and sure enough, hers had the same error, too.

Obviously there was no error, but nevertheless, I was still curious enough to ask the question anyway. So I asked, "Lord there seems to be something that You're wanting to teach me," and just as clear as anything I have ever heard, He said, "How do you sin?" I thought, uh oh! He evidently wants to change the subject. I didn't hear an audible voice (although I would love to), but it was just as clear. As I drove down the road, it dawned on me that I was having trouble answering His four word question. I thought, I sin, but I can't even tell you how. I must be so good at it that I can do it and not even know I am doing it. I must be an Olympic gold medalist sinner.

I remembered that Jesus used simple stories called parables to teach people big lessons. I would've fit right in with that crowd. So I created a parable in my mind. Let's say a man is broke and desperate. What might he say to himself? He might say, "I'm going to rob a bank and get UN-broke real quick." So in his mind's eye he starts planning the details of his heist. Thoughts like, "I'm going to wait till after dark when the guards change. I'm going to wear a mask over my face, and I'm going to wear gloves. " At some point, to actually get the cash he's got to put his hands and feet into action and follow through with the job. At that moment, I got it. We think a thought, then we see the details of how to get away with it and then we do it. Think it. See it. Do it! At that moment, I heard Him again speak , and He said, "That's right, and that's how you live free as well; that's why your enemy counterfeits it. The enemy wants you to think his thoughts so he can break into the vault of your inner man. But he's not very original. It's always been my idea for you. Troy, you learn to think like me, so you can see like me, so you can respond like me."

"Take every thought captive to the obedience of Christ." ~**2 Corinthians 10:4-5**

It's interesting that Ephesians 6, speaking of the armor of God, mentions the helmet of salvation (which is the mind of Christ). Learn to filter every thought through the mind and opinion of Christ. God can, and will, use anything and everything to bring about His character in our lives, even Bible roulette!

So far I've told you about my history and some of the things the Lord has taught me over time, but I think it's important we not confuse our history with the Lord with our testimony. They are different in many ways. Your history is more about the Lord invading your life, wooing you, drawing you to Himself, breaking your preconceived ideas about Him, and setting you free! Your testimony is all about what you can testify is true about the person Jesus. He reveals Himself and His word to you and then shows you how His love effects and deepens your everyday life with Him, setting you free!

So I want you to take a minute or two and reflect back on your history with the Lord. Now, think about what you can testify about. Pretend you are sitting on a witness stand if it helps. Think about what He has done and how these facts will effect any situation in which you might find yourself.

I want to encourage you that even if you have only known Him for a short time, you are most certainly fully equipped to have a huge impact for the kingdom. Here's proof. By design, we've talked about what some would call the basics so far. The highlights are things like our desperate need to fall in love with Him, to trust Him with every part of our lives, and that it really is all about relationship, relationship, relationship. That's a simple list, surely there's more needed to make a huge impact for Him and His kingdom?

Nope! That's it! How cool is God? Heaven, hell, and eternity hang in the balance, and God simply says that love, trust and relationship with Him are all you need.

It's just like Him to say, "I love it that you want to (represent) me to a lost and hurting world. So because I love you, I'm going to touch your lives and set you free and then I'm going to (re-present) you to that lost and hurting world."

As I was digesting these truths, the thought occurred to me, what was God's original intention? I mean, upon reflection, there were a lot of big lessons He had taught me. How do I apply them in practical application? There are a lot of ins and outs and different situations where all or some of them could apply. Hmmm, ORIGINAL INTENTION. Sounds deep and poignant, maybe God's trying to say something to me. It certainly doesn't sound like two words I would put together. So I asked, "Lord, what was your original intention?" Where would you go to find out God's original intention? Genesis, of course. So off to Genesis I went, and quickly realized that unless God wanted me to have a genealogy lesson (and I seriously hoped not), I had obviously missed something. Slowly and intently I read, hoping to see something, anything. Going back to the basics, I decided to pray. "Lord show me the meat." I'm a meat eater and not just any meat, but red meat, of the porter house T-bone variety. That is my favorite. I don't enjoy it as much as I would like. You know, that growing mid-section thing. I'm sure you understand what "show me the meat" means. It's my attempt not to use Christian-ese language or phases as often as possible. I like the inside joke feel of having secret code words with God, even though some are pretty silly and obvious, but they're still fun. I've tried, but have not always been successful, to keep a child-like simplicity to my faith.

I used to think if I didn't say a prayer just right, it wouldn't come true. Sounds more like I was trying to summon up a genie to grant me three wishes, doesn't it?

It took God six days to create everything, and I mean everything; that's saying a lot. On the seventh day He rested. My question is, why? Was He tired? What was His original intention? We all know you don't get two opportunities to make a first impression. So here it is: God made this amazing place in six days, and then, He took a day off to spend it with His son, Adam. The seventh day was Adam's first full day. I may get an argument from some theologians out there who are smarter than me, but I still believe it's true. I believe He wanted Adam's first experience with Him to be awesome. He wanted Adam's first day to be a day of peace and rest with Him. But it doesn't stop there. In case you haven't noticed, I love to reverse things. Think about it backwards. God wanted His first day with his son Adam to be a day of peace and rest. Wow, think about that; let that sink in a second. It was not only Adam's first experience with God but God's first experience with Adam in this place. I know He knew Adam before the foundation of the earth. But resist the urge to go there just yet.

I don't understand things like "before the foundation of the earth" stuff. You will lose this point if you don't keep a child-like approach. You have to place your theology, and everything else, on the sidelines for just a moment and enjoy the intimacy He's trying to express. Don't mess with it, or you'll monkey it up. Deep theological discussions don't have a place in that intimate setting.

In the beginning God created the heavens and the earth. Awesome statement, but you could also say it this way as well: In the beginning (first impression) God created intimacy and relationship with us. The Word tells us that God is the same yesterday, today and forever. So that means that His original intention for man hasn't changed either. The Lord wants us to walk with Him through our lives with peace and rest. That's not to say every day in this life is going to be a happy one. However, we can be full of joy every day. The difference between joy and happiness is that happiness depends on what is happening. Something good happens, we're happy. Something bad happens, we're unhappy. Joy doesn't care. It is constant and grounded in the Lord. The Word tells us that the joy of the Lord is our strength. So let's prove it out by reversing it. How many days of your life does the Lord want you to be weak? Zero! That means we can have joy all of the time, even if some days aren't so happy. He never promised us a rose garden, but it does mean that His desire for us is to be at peace and rest with Him.

God had prepared a perfect garden for Adam. What must that place have looked like before the fall of man? The Word tells us that God is no respecter of persons, meaning what He does for one of His kids, He's willing to do for all of His kids. The Lord prepares a garden for us as well, a garden of the heart. Adam tended his garden, and so should we.

CHAPTER 11

Intimacy Requires Brutal Honesty

Do not be deceived: God cannot be mocked. A man reaps what he sows. ~**Galatians 6:7**

Raising five children can be a daunting task. I prayed for the Lord's wisdom and revelation to be a good father. He taught me something that has become a mantra in our home. He showed me a field and told me that it's my field, and I have a say in what gets planted in it. He said this is a special field with special soil. Super soil, so to speak. He designed it that way. Whatever gets planted in it will flourish. Good seeds or bad seeds, they're going to grow. I must eat the fruit that grows in my field, rotten or ripe. Obviously, I have to be diligent about what kind of seeds get planted in the field of my heart. Sounds like a big responsibility and it is, but take heart, there's a wonderful scripture:

"Do not be deceived, God is not mocked, for whatever one sows, that will he reap."
~Galatians 6:7

At first glance it sounds ominous, but it holds a

wonderful promise. If we sow something good, God is not mocked, and He will make sure we reap something good. Gardens all have one thing in common, they all have to be tended. Adam had to tend his garden and we have to tend ours.

> *"For now we see through a glass darkly, but then face to face, now I know in part, but then shall I know even as I am known."* ~**1 Corinthians 13:12**

When would you say is a better time to tend your garden, in the middle of the day or the middle of the night? You don't have to be a rocket scientist to know tending the field of your heart is much better done in the light of day.

> *"Thy word is a lamp unto my feet and light unto my path."* ~**Psalm 119:105**

His Word lights the way to freedom and a beautiful, fruitful garden of our lives. This is not to suggest we're on our own with the heavy weight and keeping our lives right before the Lord. Remember, it's a relationship, not a dictatorship. The Lord showed me He and I walking through the garden of my life together and we came upon a plant that shouldn't be there. The Lord asked, "What's that?" Now I have a choice. I can do the Matador, which means I stand in front of it and try to distract Him to the left or the right hoping, He'll forget the question. Or, I can just keep walking, acting like I didn't hear the question. Or, I can just run from God, and unfortunately this is what we do all too often.

Sometimes in my life I will look at the Lord and say, "I'm sorry I allowed that to be planted in my life, I won't do it anymore. I'll get rid of it Lord." Then I walk over and start pulling on the weed. I usually just get blisters or worse yet, I break it off, and the root stays in the ground and will eventually grow back. So there I stood with this rotting plant in my hand and no place to put it, not a pretty sight. The Lord said, "Troy, if you will let Me, I would love to show you a better way." The Lord walks over to another weed and He bends over, grasping it and pulling, and it comes out by the root. Then He throws it as far as the East is from the West. By this point, I'm completely humbled by His grace and mercy. Like the prodigal son's father, God was expending His energy running to me, His son. As soon as the father saw His son He ran. He took action. Was the Lord of all heaven and earth just weeding my garden? Think about that, God cleaning up after me.

*"Though your sin be as scarlet, I will wash you white as snow." ~***Isaiah 1:18**

I turned and resumed our walk together and then He said, "Wait, I want to show you my favorite part." He smiled and I noticed Him reach into His pocket and take out a good seed. Bending over again, He placed it in the hole where the weed was and covered it up. As we walked on, He said, "Troy I'm not, nor have I ever been the God of change, I am the God of exchange." At that moment a picture of the cross flashed across my mind. He took what I deserve so I could have what He deserves. I had learned another huge life lesson right there in the dirt of my life. What a beautiful intimate picture He had painted for me, or should I say, He planted for me. The exchange part was amazing, but if we look a little deeper, we find that I had a very deep and lasting intimate moment with the Lord. It started with a plant that shouldn't have been there in the first place. There it is again, that anything and everything part of Himself drawing me into an ever deepening relationship, breaking my heart with how much He loves me. Me! I said through my tears, "Lord you live by a double standard, because You tell us to be good stewards of what You have given us, but You throw Your love around like it has no end."

This reminds me of a moment I had with Him a few years ago. One of my favorite hobbies is archery, any kind of archery. Bowfishing in the summer has become quite an addiction (that I never want to be healed of, I might add), and bowhunting just about anything in the winter. On one occasion, I was bowhunting whitetail deer on a ranch not far from our home. I found a great spot where the deer were crossing a creek bottom in some thick cover that happened to have a huge old oak tree about twenty yards away. *What a perfect set-up*, I thought to myself. So, I nailed a few boards in place to sit on about fifteen feet up in that amazing tree. The next morning I up in the tree there well before first light. As the sun began to rise, the scene was incredibly beautiful. Things just look different in the early morning light. Sitting there quietly for a few hours, I began to reflect on my life and relationship with the Lord, and I realized at that time in my life, I didn't feel very love sick for Him. I was comparing how I felt about Him to a feeling of being homesick I'm sure all of us have felt at least once in our lives. I know, I know, love is not a feeling, but at that moment, I became aware of something about myself that was painful to even think about. The fact was, I needed His saving love of the cross, but I wasn't in love with Him. I mean, love just for Him, not what He had done for me or could do. As I sat in that tree that winter day, I quietly whispered out loud, "Lord, I don't think that I really love You." While my words were still in the air He immediately said, "I know! But I love you, let me worry about that." In an instant I was ruined, and in love with Him. See how He is? He took me from not being in love to being deeply in love right there in that tree. I sat there weeping as quietly as I could, camo face paint streaking down my face.

I learned something that cold winter day. If I really want to know Him, the real Him, then it requires brutal honesty. Any relationship that is going to go beyond the surface and into deep intimacy has got to be honest, and that my friend, is non-negotiable. Think about the word intimacy. Now, say it really slow a couple of times. It starts to sound like "into me see" doesn't it? It's one thing to know the Lord sees the inner most workings of who you are, but it's another thing entirely to invite Him behind the veil of who you are. I didn't get a deer that day, but it was still another divine great set-up.

CHAPTER 12

Encourage Yourself!

*But the one who prophesies speaks to people for
their strengthening, encouraging and comfort.*
~1 Corinthians 14:3

Occasionally over the years, I noticed the Lord
would send someone to encourage me on my journey.
Sometimes it was right before I would need it, and at
other times, I was at the breaking point when I received
it.

On one occasion, I was driving from our home
in Kerrville to Austin, Texas, which is about two hours
away, to pick up a new bowfishing boat. I was so
excited because this was a big upgrade. My old boat
had so many leaks in it that I had to turn on the bilge
pump at least once every hour just to keep it on the lake
instead of in the lake. Even though this was an exciting
day for me, it was also the first time in a while that I
had been alone. During the drive I began to notice my
inner man had a few leaks as well. It was a day of more
than one kind of upgrade. As I drove, I recognized I
was more than a little frustrated in my life, and it

seemed all that I had done for a long time was encourage people, but I hadn't been encouraged in a long time. In retrospect, I was being a pouting baby, crying for my bottle of milk. I didn't see it right away, but the Lord was serving up my favorite, porter house T-bone. As I drove and complained He interrupted me with a stern "YOU DO IT!" You do it? Where did that come from and what did that mean? He dropped one of His little pebbles into my inner man, and suddenly I knew what He meant. I slowly glanced up and to my right to move my rearview mirror into place so I could look myself in the eye as I encouraged myself; the mirror was already aligned perfectly. I'm not saying He moved it into perfect alignment so I would be staring right into my own eyes. I had been on the road for over an hour and hadn't noticed it, but I'm not saying that He didn't move it either.

I began looking back and forth from the road ahead and then back into the mirror as I encouraged myself. Encouraging turned into rebuking, rebuking turned to preaching, and preaching turned into freedom. I had received a big upgrade. I had learned to encourage myself and learned to remind myself of what I believed. I mean, who better to pray for me than me? He is never late, but He sure ain't early either. I guess that's the nature of perfect timing. These words of encouragement were life to my whole being. I began to find myself wanting to do the same thing for other people. After all, that's how the economy of God works. You get more of what you give away. I noticed I was being drawn to people with an encouraging word, usually sharing what the Lord had shown me about Himself and how sufficient and efficient He is to meet all of our needs.

As I stepped into the deeper waters of my faith, I began to exercise my faith to a degree that my flesh was a bit uncomfortable. Faith is sometimes spelled "RISK." I realized that the Lord began to move on my heart for people, and I would seem to get a real sense of how they felt deep inside. I could almost feel their struggle as I prayed, but as I felt these things with them, I also had a stronger sense of the Lord's provision for them. My favorite part of this process was encouraging people to believe God, not just in Him, exposing their issues to the truths He had placed in me. I would tell them about His crazy love for them and how much He is for them and help them put their lives into perspective in the light of His heart for them, much like he had done for me.

During these times, it became obvious He was using me prophetically. In the beginning, it was just small encouragements. Then, it began to build into something more. I would just know stuff about people and my prayers for them became very specific. This started to freak me out a little bit; I mean, I was prophesying into lives. I thought that was stuff for people who really had it going on with God, those gifted individuals who had been grounded in the Lord and His Word for many, many years. I needed to see for myself what scripture had to say about prophecy. I read in 1 Corinthians 14:

"But the one who prophesies speaks to people for

their strengthening, encouraging and comfort.'
~1 Corinthians 14:3

Other versions of the word say it this way, *"Edification, comfort and exhortation."* Simply put, if I feed you the truth and comfort you with facts and encourage you to believe and apply them to your life, then I have just prophesied to you, according to 1 Corinthians 14:3.

I realize that often the Lord will give us facts about someone's past, present or future to validate what He has us say. In the light of scripture, this didn't sound so unreasonable or out of bounds for me after all. I have grown to love encouraging people in the Lord. As a matter of fact, it's my favorite thing to do. This is the normal progression of things in the Spirit, to see others blessed and changed as they learn to trust Him with their lives. This, like God Himself, is just supernaturally normal. My experience with the Lord has always felt very normal. That is not to say at times it wasn't dramatic, over the top and very intense, but sometimes that is what it feels like to be moved from a false and totally bankrupt mindset into the light of His liberating presence.

Just because something feels foreign to us doesn't mean it's not how it was intended to be. Make no mistake, it is God's intent we encourage each other, edify each other and strengthen each other. How better than to be in love with God and our fellow man than being empowered by the Holy Spirit through prophecy. I used to think that prophecy and other gifts were something you earned through long study and powerful mentorship and if you were successful, then and only then, could you attain the high and lofty goal of moving in the prophetic. This of course is bologna. Here's proof in 1 Corinthians. Paul said, "I wish that you all prophesied." Why would he say that if it was almost impossible to grasp? In my experience, as the Lord began to use me to speak into lives prophetically, I loved it. It was so awesome to be a part of seeing the Lord touching people through me, but after a few years I noticed that it wasn't much fun anymore. Some people began to expect me to have a word ready to go, and at the same time, I began to prophesy for prophesy's sake, and that is a recipe for burn out. The Lord didn't let it go that far; He simply asked me a question. He asked, "Why do you think this prophecy thing feels like work to you now? " I've been around long enough to know that when He asks a question, He's not really in need of an answer, but instead wants to give one. He said, "Troy you have lost sight of why you prophecy, and which is because I love them, and I want you to agree with me and love them too." There it was, pure, life-changing truth wrapped up in one simple sentence.

"If I have the gift of prophecy and can fathom all mysteries and all knowledge, and if I have faith that can move mountains, but have not love, I am nothing." ~**1 Corinthians 13:2**

I began to understand that I had let what the Lord called me to do change what He had called me to be. We are human beings, not human doings.

It is very important to follow the Lord into what He has called you to do, but we cannot lose sight of the fact that its power rests in our intimacy with Him and what He has first called us to be. He is not looking for warriors, preachers, teachers, missionaries etc., etc., etc. He's looking for lovers of God, just for Him. The only thing the enemy is really intimidated by is your intimacy with the King, not your gifts or even your knowledge of the Word. He knows that's where the real destructive power to his evil kingdom comes from. When the Lord, as in the Ezekiel 37 vision of the valley of dry bones, breathes life into us and we agree with it and apply its truths, we will be freed and raised up into an exceedingly great army, and we will crush anything that raises itself up against the knowledge of God.

"So shall they fear the name of the Lord from the West, and his glory from the rising of the sun. When the enemy comes in like a flood, the spirit of the Lord will lift up a standard against him."
~Isaiah 59:19

The first time I read this, the picture in my imagination was a flood of the enemy coming at us and the Lord raising a dam of protection. Upon doing a little snooping around, a very different picture began to come into focus. You see, the word standard means a marching banner of war. When the enemy comes in like a flood, the Spirit of the Lord raises an offensive, marching banner of war. In ancient times, a banner or standard often declared who you were and what your intentions were. It is of the utmost importance we decide who we are (and by decide I really mean 'agree' with the Lord about who He says we are) and what our intentions are. Soldiers say, "Do we have to go to war?" Warriors say, "When do we get to go to war?" That's just an old saying of course. But this attitude can be found all over the Bible. Take a look at 1 Samuel 17:

"Your servant has killed both the lion and the bear. This uncircumcised Philistine (Goliath) will be like one of them because he has defied the armies of the living God." ~**1 Samuel 17:36**

In light of this scripture, consider King David's mighty men. I'm not saying they were the most stable guys in the world, which may be why I love them so much. During peace time one of them asked for a vacation, so to speak, and took off on a journey to Ethiopia because he'd heard there were still some giants left over there. He went on a mission to pick a fight with the biggest one he could find because he wanted to be like his king. On another occasion, one of them was walking from one town to the next and happened upon a lion trap. A lion pit was a huge pit with steep walls, camouflaged over with sticks and branches and then baited. When a lion fell in, it couldn't get out, and then could be killed with a bow and arrow or a spear from a safe distance with little risk. Well, this soldier was just on the road by himself and came upon a pit with a lion in it. With no one rooting him on and no peer pressure, he decided it would be a good idea to jump down into the pit with the lion and kill it, just so he could be like his king.

I'm not advocating pickin' fights with giants or jumping into lion pits, but you have to love a heart that wants to conquer some of the same things as the king. They say imitation is the greatest compliment one can receive. The Word tells us the greatest commandment is to love the Lord your God with all your heart and all your soul and with all your mind, and the second greatest is like it, love your neighbor as yourself. But the commandment spoken more often than any other is, do not fear, but instead be brave and courageous, or some variation of that. I haven't counted, but I've heard many times that it's mentioned 365 times, once for every day of the year. I wouldn't doubt it, given how much encouragement we humans seem to need concerning this issue. He understands when some of His children decide to agree with Him about who He says they are that His light illuminates their inadequacies and frailties. This can be a big problem if we lose sight of the fact that scripture teaches us in our weakness He is made strong. I believe that is one of the reasons He commands, not suggests, we do not lose heart but instead remain brave and courageous. It is simply our choice to focus on the promise and not the problem.

Speaking of focus, one of the most liberating moments for me was when the Lord opened my eyes to the red letter scripture in John 5:

"Very truly I tell you, the son can do nothing by

*himself, he can do only what he sees his father
doing, because whatever the father does the son
also does." ~***John 5:19***

If the Lord Jesus can do nothing except what He sees someone else doing (His Father), then He wasn't kidding when He said that He came to this earth 100% man. He is the perfect example of man in right relationship with God, a picture of what it looks like to live in God's original intention on the earth, even after the fall of man in the book of Genesis. For me, it's liberating because if Jesus could do nothing except what He saw, then it's obvious to me He is trying to teach me how important it is to see Him. Seeing life through the filter of the mind of Christ, having wisdom and understanding and walking in intimate relationship, not only fosters an ever deepening relationship with Him, but it is extremely dangerous to the enemy's strongholds wherever we find them, and find them we will.

The longer I walk with Him, the more I have come to understand how ready and willing He is to share His ways with us and how supernaturally normal He wants our lives to be. What would it look like if we really, really believed Him? If these things were hard to understand and complicated to operate, then He owes the guys in Luke 9:40-41 an apology. Here was a desperate father whose son was possessed by a demon. Upon bringing his son to Jesus he says, "I begged your disciples to drive it out, but they could not." "You unbelieving and perverse generation," Jesus replied,

"How long shall I stay with you and put up with you?" Ouch! It would be reasonable to think the disciples might say to themselves, "Wow! Jesus, that's pretty harsh, I mean we're talk'n demon possession here!" But Jesus, just callin' it as He SEES it, rebuked their belief system. Commonly phrased, He rebuked their unbelief.

To tell you the truth, I'm not sure what it was, but I do know there are two totally different dynamics at play in most of our lives. On one hand, we may be in a place of genuine unbelief, or on the other hand, we may be in a place of choosing not to agree with what the Lord says about who we are in Him. This, I can tell you from experience, is a great subject to pray about; the Lord loves us to ask His opinion about adjustments in our thinking. Most of the time it's as simple as making fine tuning adjustments. Let's say you are driving down the road, and your radio just sounds like static coming from the speakers. What would you do? You would very gently adjust the tuner up or down a very small amount and shazam! Everything starts coming through clearly. That's how a lot of things are with the Lord - simple. See, from His view point it's normal, natural and just plain common sense for demons to obey in His name. In Luke 10:17-20 the seventy-two returned with joy and said, "Lord, even the demons submit to us in your name." He replied, "I saw Satan fall like lightning from heaven. I have given you authority to trample on snakes and scorpions and to overcome all the power of the enemy, nothing will harm you. However, do not rejoice that the spirits submit to you, but rejoice that your names are written in heaven." Other translations replace the word rejoice with marvel or amazement. In other words, Jesus says it's not even news worthy to mention that demons are subject to us. That's red letter, folks. (Red letter: The spoken words of Jesus in the Bible.)

The things that we (choose) to believe, the things we (choose) to think, the way we (choose) to see things, the way we (choose) to see ourselves, all effect what we do in our lives. The Lord's heart and mind for each of His children is that we (choose) to believe like Him, to think, see and do just like He does. However we should take it a step further and say to ourselves, the enemy, and even a lost and hurting world that the Spirit of the living God lives inside of me and He expects me to conquer.

The Lord wants His unreasonable love and confidence to become such a part of who we are that we long to wield His words in power, pulling down strongholds. It was through His love and mercy that God Himself, Richard and Latriece (Thunder Finger) Harper had pursued me, and found it just unreasonable that I spend my life away from His truth.

I have found this heart attitude and mindset contagious. These people, and others I have known through the years truly enjoy being a part of what God is doing in and around them, to the point they are deeply effected seeing what He can do in the lives of others. We have joined them on the journey to reveal Jesus to a world that is in desperate need of knowing how loved they are, right where they are.

CHAPTER 13

Be Supernaturally Normal!

Very truly I tell you, whoever believes in me will do the works I have been doing, and they will do even greater things than these, because I am going to the Father. ~**John 14:12**

It has been a great pleasure and treasure to be in relationship with some pretty amazing people, one of which is Bill Johnson, a pastor and international speaker, among other things. I love Bill for many reasons, not the least of which is that he likes to hunt, fish and enjoy bar-b-q almost as much as I do. When I am around Bill, I have gleaned to keep my ears open. It's in those moments that I have learned some very important lessons like THE HOLY SPIRIT IS IMPRISONED INSIDE THE BODIES of UN-BELIEVING BELIEVERS AND HE WANTS OUT. Obviously, he wasn't talking about imprisonment, but instead our need to believe God in our everyday walk with Him. We need to learn to show the world that the impossible is nothing for God. Balance in Christian life isn't going to church on Sunday, a mid-week fill-up at a home group later in the week, or even personal Bible study. Those things are great and needed, but God wants us to agree with His heart for this world, unleash Him out of our inner man and watch Him accomplish the impossible in our everyday life.

Randy Clark once said he longs for the time when the Bride of Christ raises the dead with monotonous regularity. It sounds way out there until you read it in the light of John 14.

"Very truly I tell you, whoever believes in me will do the works I have been doing, and they will do even greater things than these, because I am going to the father." ~**John 14:12**

Some would say that He was speaking of salvation and evangelism because He came to seek and to save the lost through the redeeming power of His shed blood on the cross, and they would be right. But this scripture plainly says whoever believes will do the same things that He had been doing, and greater. Those aren't my words and they are not your words, they are His words, and He's not going to repent or apologize for saying them. The question is, will His bride believe and agree with His Word to us or are we going to continue to dribble on about how unworthy or ill-equipped we are or some other bunch of bologna? Step out of your comfort zone and pray, and while you're at it, choose to believe Him and not just in Him. After all, it's just His supernaturally normal original intention.

CHAPTER 14

A Miracle On The Battlefield Of The Mind

Time to apply what you believe.

Sometimes in our lives we are required to appropriate all that He has taught us and agree with Him by applying the truth of His Word to our situation. In other situations, we are to stand our ground by focusing on the promise instead of the problem and allow the Lord to move on our behalf. Over the last few years, we have found ourselves in both of these situations, and both situations were extreme from my point of view.

The first occurred in 2007 when Michelle needed to have a hysterectomy, which is a major surgery, however very common with a low-level risk factor. As a matter of fact, there is less than 10% chance of major or even minor complications. So I wasn't too stressed about it after I was convinced of that fact, of course I wasn't the one having surgery Michelle was, but she seemed ready to get it behind her. We decided to schedule the procedure in early November of that year, three of our five children have birthdays in and around the holiday season plus Thanksgiving, Christmas and New Year's. I don't think we had too much time to get too nervous over the impending surgery anyway.

The day of the surgery was upon us before we knew it. Michelle, just being Michelle, had all of the birthday and Christmas shopping completely done and saw to it that the troops (the kids and me) were rallied to decorate the house with all of our fall decor. It seemed like everything was ready so we could really enjoy the holiday season without any last minute chaos. Everything was going smoothly. This is the part I call "the calm before the storm". Little did I know God was about to require me to appropriate almost everything I knew about His ways in the battlefield of the mind.

The alarm clock went off at 3:30 a.m. so we would have enough time to make the one hour drive to the hospital, check-in and have Michelle prepped for surgery. As is usually the case before surgery, sleep was almost non-existent. However, God gave us a verse for that in Philippians:

"I can do all things through Christ who strengthens me." ~**Philippians 4:13**

I had no idea early that morning I would need to apply this scripture and many others before the day was over. I also had no idea I would go to sleep that night a different person, forever changed, but again God is not the God of change. He is the God of *exchange*. That day, He would be in the business of putting teeth to my gospel, training me on the battlefield, teaching me the truth of scripture, specifically the scripture that says we can speak life or death, blessing or curse. It was high time I became a meat-eating son and no longer be satisfied with just milk. You see, it would be a day of hunting the foe of my mind and putting him down. This would not be a day of skimming the cream off the top of what someone else had churned for me.

Some of you no doubt have similar stories of your own, and as you're going to read my story you will love it and rejoice with me. However, some of you will not understand it or see how it fits in with what you currently believe about God; and some of you are not going to dig it at all. I only ask that you would pray about these things and weigh what is written with the Word of God.

So, it was 4:30 a.m. and Michelle and I were headed to the hospital. I soon noticed that she was feeling a little apprehensive, which was very understandable, so we prayed together. I felt moved by God to tell her the story of Gehazi in 2 Kings 6:17. She had heard it before, but sometimes it's comforting to hear someone else tell about the Lord's exploits. The story is about Gehazi the servant of Elisha. A vast enemy army had surrounded God's people in the middle of the night. When Gehazi woke up the next morning, he stepped out of his tent and was in total terror, and ran to Elisha saying, "What are we going to do?" Basically, Gehazi was freakin' out because this huge army had surrounded them and obviously had an extreme advantage because they were tactically superior and larger in number. So Elisha said, "Hey, relax dude, it's okay. We've got more guys on our side than they do on their side." Then he asked the Lord to open Gehazi's eyes to see what was really happening. The Lord opened Gehazi's eyes, and he saw a vast and mighty army of the Lord riding fiery chariots. Instantly he went from saying, "There is no way we can survive," to saying, "There is no way they can survive." Gehazi had a paradigm shift, meaning he exchanged one way of thinking for a correct way of thinking because he saw the truth and was no longer deceived by his perception.

Upon arriving at the hospital we prayed again, and I could tell she had something on her mind, which I just dismissed as part of the situation. I would find out later that I had been mistaken. We went inside to check-in and the staff took her to prep for surgery, and just that quickly she was gone.

The average hysterectomy takes about forty-five minutes to complete. The nursing staff said they would come and get me when she was in recovery. We would spend the night at the hospital and be home the following afternoon. As I waited downstairs in the main lobby of the hospital, intently watching the clock on the wall, I began to feel my prayers change for Michelle. I assumed it was just my desire to get word that the procedure had gone well. Almost exactly on time a nurse appeared and said that Michelle was in recovery and I could go upstairs to be with her. When I arrived at her room, she was lying in her bed and seemed comfortable, although she was still unconscious. Going through my mental check list she looked very pale, but that was to be expected. Her heart rate on the monitor looked low and so did her blood pressure, but she had always had low blood pressure. My optimism could explain all of these things away. After all, she had just had surgery.

I stood near the doorway to make room for the four nurses attending Michelle, but I could see that something wasn't right. The look of concern on their faces and the fact they didn't acknowledge me as I entered the room told me all was not well. Then one of the nurses pulled the sheet down to Michelle's ankles, and the bed was full of blood. The head nurse then asked me to wait in the hallway, which I completely disregarded. I wasn't going anywhere. They somewhat lifted Michelle to remove the bloody sheets and quickly replaced them with clean ones. Later I learned this was done to assess if the blood was just temporary and had stopped on its own or if not, to determine how much she was bleeding. Two nurses put the bloody sheets in a clear plastic bag and placed it under a counter near the back of the room. The head nurse looked at the clock on the wall as she covered Michelle back up and then placed two warming blankets on her. I will never forget the solemn looks of concern on their faces as I stood there in shock. At that moment, the surgeon walked in and instantly the head nurse pulled back the sheet to reveal as much new blood as there had been only minutes before. The doctor looked at me and said, "There's a lot of blood, but sometimes is to be expected." I looked at the him and pointed to the clear plastic bag with the first set of bloody sheets in it and demanded, "What about that?" I watched as panic appeared in his eyes. He immediately began directing his team move her back into surgery. And just like that she was gone again.

I raced into the downstairs lobby with cell phone in hand desperate to get a signal. I was finally able to make contact with a few friends and family members and asked them to pray. "Please call everyone you know to pray, and pray right now!" I begged. A floor nurse stayed with me on the trip downstairs to the lobby area; I'm sure I looked terrified and confused. Once there, she said someone would update me on Michelle's condition as soon as possible. I looked at the clock, marking the time. I rationalized if the complete surgery had taken forty-five minutes, then correcting the problem should take much less.

The floor of the lobby was stained concrete surrounded by carpeted areas with chairs. I found myself in the middle of the large concrete area walking in a circle about fifteen feet in circumference. I didn't know why, but I walked that a circle praying nonstop. I don't mind telling you, I was scared. I mean *really* scared. This was Michelle, my wife, the mother of our five children, and my best friend on earth. Last and very least, she was my business partner. I could not imagine life without her. These were the thoughts that ran screaming through my mind as I walked in a circle. "I need Jesus, the real Jesus, and I need him right now, and by now, I mean NOW!" As I walked, it was as if I would pass through a veil, like a doorway into a different realm and stay there while I was on one side of the circle. I would have thoughts like, *How am I going to go home and look into my eight year old daughters eyes and tell her that mommy isn't coming home?* Then, as if passing through another veil on the other side of the circle, I would have thoughts like, *This isn't going to happen. God's got this. Everything is going to be all right.* Then through the other veil again, thoughts of walking through life without her terrified me to the point I thought I would throw up. This scene played out for several minutes, and I knew every minute was very important.

Finally, I abruptly stopped and said, "Lord teach me!" That's all, just Lord teach me. At that instant, I had a sense that He was there and had been there all along. (Call it a revelation; call it whatever you want, but it was very clear to my inner man that He was there with me, waiting and listening.) I knew He was standing right behind me and to the right, flanking me as I walked. I took a slow step forward fighting my thoughts, intently listening for His voice. I knew He was walking as well. A picture flashed into my mind of a football quarterback of being called to the sideline to have a conference with his coach. The coach asked passionately, "What do you think you're doing? We've gone over and over this in practice, what do you want me to do, go out there and throw the ball for you? Now get back out there and do your job, man!" I don't mind telling you I was shocked by this picture of a coach and quarterback, and at that moment I sure didn't want to be the quarterback. Come to think of it, I really didn't want to be the coach either. If anything, I thought I needed him to step out onto that field and throw the ball for me. As I walked through the veils, I recognized one side as the valley of the shadow of death, and the other side as mountain top moments of confidence in God. Try to understand these two different sides of this circle, one horrific and one wonderful; it's easy to understand each in different times and seasons of our lives. But as a rule, we seem to find ourselves in one or the other after months and months in our everyday lives. Life has ups and downs, but I was going from being immersed in one season to being immersed in the center of another season within an instant.

I began to pray *hard*, if you know what I mean. I threw every scripture I could think of in shotgun fashion at the situation. I shoveled every testimony I had ever heard onto the problem. Then a soft gentle voice broke through my mind, and I heard Him say, "Troy, listen to me. I am sufficient and efficient to meet all of your needs." I responded, "I know Lord, and I thank you and praise you for that." As I was still speaking, He continued His sentence that I had obviously interrupted and said, "NO MATTER WHAT HAPPENS." *Had I heard right? Did He just say, I am sufficient and efficient to meet all of your needs, no matter what happens.* Shock and fear slapped me across the face, and I stopped and blurted out, "What in the hell does that mean? 'No matter what happens!' Don't you know?", I screamed on the inside. He gently replied, "Son, I don't know what you are going to choose to agree with right now." He was saying there were two different roads to travel. One was a trail where He would be with me no matter how bleak the situation, and the other was something else. It was a decision to believe God and to stand up and speak like a son, full of His very available power... to declare the Lord's Lordship over and into Michelle's body in the here and the now... to punish the enemy and his plans for us on the battlefield of this moment... to grow up and finally start to believe God and not just in Him... to pick up my weapon that He had given me and load it with truth and use it to put down this giant. Please don't misunderstand me here; I'm using words like enemy, battlefield, weapon etc., but this wasn't about my power, it was about a birth. It was as if I was a woman in the throes of transition, while at the same time, I was the child being born. God was delivering me into the knowledge that my identity in Him is the foundation for excellence through Him. As I prayed and declared life as I walked, I noticed that both sides of the circle were now light and full of UN-natural peace.

"Be anxious for nothing, but in everything by prayer and supplication with thanksgiving let your request be made known to God. And the peace of God which surpasses all comprehension, will guard your hearts and your minds in Christ Jesus. Finally, brethren, whatever is true, whatever is honorable, whatever is right, whatever is lovely, whatever is of good repute, if there is any excellence and if anything worthy of praise, dwell on these things."
~Philippians 4:6-8

The valley of the shadow of death was gone. Echoing in my spirit were the words whispered by the Lord, "I have given you power to speak life and death, blessing or a curse and I do not apologize." In other words, apply the truth through agreement and do what I have taught you. Or, using the Lord's football metaphor, run the play and throw the ball and trust THE receiver, He will be there, and a touchdown is imminent.

Whether I liked it or not, I had a responsibility in this amazing relationship. My mind had been assaulted, both by the enemy of my soul and the Lover of it. The enemy dared me to stay in the comfort zone I had built for myself, rooms full of casual Christianity and a pantry full of personal theology that just didn't have much power, but the Lord was having none of it, so He burned it down.

I remembered many years before a prophetic word I received from a man who I respected very much. I had forgotten it until that moment. He said, "The Lord is going to train you on the battlefield. He has given you a sword and He says He's not going to swing it for you." Suddenly, feeling full of power and determination, I turned and found myself running toward a set of electronic hospital doors, the kind that are kept locked. They weren't; opening the doors, I raced a three-way intersection of hallways. Being led by the Holy Spirit, I turned to the right, moving quickly. I soon came to another set of doors that appeared to be locked, but I pushed them anyway and they opened. I walked straight ahead about twenty or thirty steps to a third set of doors, pushing them open as well. Not one door was closed to me. Maybe it was a coincidence that all three sets of magnetically locked security doors were left unlocked. What do you think?

I stood in a big room with curtains covering the individual rooms, much like an I.C.U. A nurse sitting at a desk in front of me never looked up. I turned to my right and took a step, but strangely stopped and turned back to my left. I opened the first curtain I came to and found my wife lying unconscious in a dimly lit room. The surgeon was standing on the left side of her bed with one hand covering his mouth. He stared at Michelle and watched her monitor. As I entered the shock in his eyes, confirmed that I had gained access beyond what was normally allowed. Stuttering he said, "I can't do anything... I can't do anything. She's not stable. I can't put her back under until she stabilizes." He was talking as much to convince himself as he was to convince me. I looked at him and without thinking asked, "Do you love your wife?" Dumbfounded by the question he asked, "What did you say?" I repeated, "Do you love your wife?" He replied simply, "Yes." Then I looked at him, pointed my finger and said, "Then you do for mine what you would do for yours, and you do it right now!"

Now don't get me wrong, I wasn't telling him what to do because I didn't know what to do, and he could have already been doing all the right things. But he moved quickly past me to the nurses' station. He could've been calling security for all I knew. He reached over the counter and retrieved a clipboard and thrusting it at me said to fill it out. He then moved quickly to a phone on the wall and gave orders to the nurse behind the counter. As he walked past me I said, "I can't even see what's written on this sheet of paper, much less clearly think enough to fill this thing out." He hesitated and knowing the stress I was under, said something like, numbers 4, 7 and 12 are "yes," and the rest are "no". I quickly filled out the form, and handed it to him. He gave me a solemn look and said, "Go back to the waiting area."

I returned to the all too familiar waiting area but this time I was a different person. I had a sense that I had been confronted by my enemy on the battlefield, and I had won. I had known the Lord as savior and the lover of my soul. I had known Him as King and Lord of all, but that day I came to know Him as coach. The Lord had taken pleasure in seeing me walk into this hospital a child, and in some ways, I would walk out a believing son. Another forty-five minutes would go by until I would be reunited with Michelle. She didn't have just one bleed, but three, and it was proven that the surgeon made the right decision to go back in when he did.

After we got home Michelle told me there was a moment right before we left for the hospital early that morning, she looked into her closet at all of the Christmas presents and all the preparation she had done for our family, and had a strange sense she would not come home from the hospital. She said it wasn't a fearful thought, just a knowing.

This was a tough chapter for me to write, mainly because I find it much easier to talk about my failures than I do about my successes. I also struggled with how to tell one story and still be sensitive to some people who might read it and have been in a similar situation that didn't turn out the same way. Please understand, He is the God of all our situations, whether they turn out the way we want or not. There is no formula that works to get the desired result we may want all of the time. Our lives are made up of events and situations in the process of life that work together to create a huge beautiful tapestry called YOU. This was a story of His mercy and faithfulness to teach me His mind and heart in that moment. It was also a harsh reminder that it is important to believe and apply what and who God says I am and the unchanging need for His bride to agree with His ways. It's interesting that the scripture in Philippians 4:6-8 starts with a command to #1 be anxious for nothing, #2 pray and give thanks, #3 then a guard will be placed over your heart and mind, #4 making you able to think like the Lord. It is putting on the mind of Christ, which is the helmet of salvation. In other words, it's the protection for your mind that saves. Remember Jesus said in John 5:

> *"I tell you the truth, the son of man can do nothing by himself, he can do only what he sees the father doing, because whatever the father does the son also does."* ~**John 5:19**

When I was walking in that horrific yet wonderful circle in the hospital lobby and I said the words "teach me", He allowed me to see His heart in that situation and encouraged me to speak His words of life into it, all the way to the end zone, with heavenly hosts and hounds of hell watching. He was and is faithful to teach and to train His children to overcome the enemy by the blood of the Lamb and the word of their testimony, applying truth in the process of life that sets us free.

This chapter was about the Lord's desire to train and equip His children to become sons and daughters, applying His heart and mind to any and all situations in which we find ourselves. It was about His heart to do great exploits in and through His kids, and I am no exception. The next chapter is also about His amazing love and power but in a completely different way. It was the catalyst that inspired me to write this book in the first place. It was by far the most difficult and wonderful time of our lives. The whole event was a contradiction, as it was both agonizing and awesome. I never ever want to go through anything even remotely like it again. But at the same time, the miracles we saw were life changing and we will never be the same.

CHAPTER 15

The Impossible Is Nothing To God

Even though I walk through the darkest valley, I will fear no evil, for you are with me; your rod and your staff, they comfort me. You prepare a table before me in the presence of my enemies. You anoint my head with oil; my cup overflows.
~Psalm 23:4-5

God used Michelle's life to teach me how to apply and believe the truth of His Word. He would use the life of my daughter, Maggie, to teach me how to stand on the ground of His promises.

July 3rd, 2011, near seven in the evening my phone rang. It would be the most life altering call of our lives. Maggie's friend, Olivia, was screaming into the phone, "Mr. Faust, we've been in an accident, Maggie's been ejected, she's unconscious, she's breathing, I think." Then the call was dropped.

The top of my head started tingling, which turned to stinging as I ran to the driveway behind Michelle. It felt like my eyes were being pushed out from the inside, and I could not focus them. Everything seemed blurry. My breathing was deep and hard. Michelle was screaming and crying and praying through her tears as I tried to back out of our driveway. As I drove down the driveway, which is about two hundred and fifty yards long, I thought I was having an issue with my hearing. I had heard of people having strange physical issues when under extreme stress. I thought the radio was on, and the last thing we wanted was to listen to music. I reached for the tuner on the radio, and it was already off. Confused, I glanced at Michelle, and the look on her face was one that I will never forget. I knew she needed me to hold it together, but as I looked at her, I was very confused because her screams would fade in and out being muted by the music. I could hear her scream, but the next second I could hear singing. All this happened before we could even get out of our driveway. Was I in shock, was I having a stroke or heart attack?

Then something happened I couldn't explain. I noticed the singing that had been confusing me was coming from me. That's right, I was singing, and I don't sing, ever! Let's just say I have a voice only a parent would love, so I don't sing unless I'm singing to the Lord. Nevertheless, I was singing. The song coming out of my mouth was one we had sung at church only a few times in the past. The words are: "You are good, your love lasts forever, we will rest in your unfailing love, consume our praise with fire down from heaven, and fill our lives with power from above." I don't know the rest of the words, but I sang those words to the Lord for the next several days. I didn't do much else. I prayed, but this thing with the singing shocked me, and it was obvious the Holy Spirit had initiated it. It was surreal; my daughter had just been in an accident bad enough to eject her from the vehicle. Her friend at the scene didn't know whether or not she was alive. I couldn't focus my eyes. My wife was screaming, but her voice was fading in and out, and I was trying to drive to the scene, all while my imagination was running totally out of control. And I'm singing, really! I was losing it, I mean people do snap sometimes. Singing! I just couldn't believe I was singing a worship song. The last thing on my mind was worshipping. Praying yes, scream praying absolutely, but worshipping, no. I was losing it, that was a fact, but what was "IT"?

All of this happened before we left our property. I knew where the kids had been, so finding the accident was easy. Driving down the road thoughts flooded my mind. *How is this real? How is Michelle going to deal with my medical event in the midst of all this hell? I've got to focus, but I can hardly see to drive. I can't fail her. Get under control!* Then I noticed that I was singing even louder. I'd been in this rodeo long enough to know that control was not something I really wanted. God is always in control no matter what we think or believe. Sure we have free will, but this place and all places were His. Period.

I wanted to stand up and help my family, stand for what I believed in and fight like I had been taught not that long ago. Standing and proclaiming seemed easy looking back on that hospital lobby. This was my baby girl; I'd been protecting her since birth. This wasn't about fighting; this was about standing and believing. Evidently, this was about worship as well. My mind didn't know what to do... pray, fight, stand, proclaim, declare, curse, bless, blah, blah, blah. I didn't care, just as long as it would move the hand of God to help my daughter now, right now. There was that manipulation thing, I would do anything to save my daughter, and I didn't care if I did it the right way or the wrong way. This was war, but I didn't feel like I could handle anything that even remotely looked like war. However, I had been taught that He expected things from me, didn't He? I was a son taught to speak and to attack the enemy. If ever I found myself in a situation like this, I was to believe God and to put down my enemies. He was my Father and had taught me, so what was I doing so fragile and broken, again? But there I was, worshipping and driving the six or seven miles to my daughter.

Somehow we made it to the scene of Maggie's accident. I pulled the car over to the side of the road behind a long line of vehicles that had already stopped. Michelle was out of the vehicle in an instant, before it was even stopped; she was running. No care for what she might find, but sprinting to our daughter. I pitied anyone or anything that got in her way, including the peace officer who tried to stop her. She broke free of his grasp and continued to run. A Life Flight helicopter was landing, two ambulances were already at the scene, and a crowd of spectators had gathered. As we arrived, paramedics were lifting Maggie onto a stretcher, she was in and out of consciousness. There is no feeling so excruciating as standing over your bloody and broken child being loaded into a helicopter.

The accident happened on a curvy country road that had a long straight away with a series of deep blind dips going downhill in one section. It was known by some of the local teenagers as the "fun road", and not for its scenic views. If you've ever experienced what it feels like to go speeding through a dip on a country road, then you know the sensation you feel in the pit of your stomach. Imagine a series of dips in rapid succession at a downhill angle with a sixteen year old teenager driving with four of her friends in the car, and you start to get the picture. Common sense is replaced by exhilaration, and prudence replaced by acceleration.

Going into the third and last rollercoaster-like dip, the right rear tire left the road and landed in the soft dirt at the edge of the road. We believe she over corrected to the left and shot across the road at a high rate of speed; the impact with the tree line on the opposite side of the road was inevitable. In an instant, her 2006 Chevrolet Trailblazer went end over end once and then flipped violently down the asphalt hill three and a half more times. Maggie was the only one to be ejected from the vehicle. Her body hit the asphalt about twenty feet from the Trailblazer, which rested on its side. I have been in the automobile business for many, many years and I couldn't have told you what kind of vehicle it was at first glance, had I not already known. The destruction was massive. For reasons I don't know, neither of the two front airbags ever deployed. Two of the four teenagers left the scene with their parents, uninjured. The other two went to the hospital to be checked out with minor injuries and went home later that night. This was nothing short of a miracle.

Neither Michelle nor I were allowed to ride with Maggie on the helicopter, and although the life-flight would only take thirty minutes or less, the drive to the hospital in san Antonio would take us at least an hour. Our son, Matt, joined us at the accident scene and rode with us in the backseat. We drove away as soon as the rotors on the helicopter began to spin, but we knew we wouldn't be at the hospital with Maggie when she arrived. She would be alone. Driving away, Michelle couldn't take her eyes off the helicopter until it faded out of sight, and then she threw up.

Our youngest daughter, Samantha was at youth group when she received the call. I hated being separated from Sam knowing how badly she would need us, but we had no time to waste. The youth pastor, who is also my nephew, offered to drive Samantha to the hospital. As they left the youth chapel, Maggie's helicopter flew overhead, and Sam began to pray and weep for the life of her sister.

Hannah, our second daughter was on her way to a summer job in Nashville when she heard about the accident. Although she was still on the ground in San Antonio, her plane had already left the terminal and they would not allow her to exit the aircraft. Hannah would have to make the flight to Nashville knowing only that her sister had been in a horrible accident and was getting life-flighted to a major hospital.

Megan, our oldest daughter stayed behind at the

scene until the helicopter flew away. She told us later that after Michelle and I left for the hospital, the helicopter doors flew open and a paramedic began urgently asking for Maggie's parents. She had gone into respiratory distress and they needed permission to intubate her, which is the first step to resuscitate a trauma victim. Megan told them we had left for the hospital, but to do whatever they had to do. As they shut the doors again the last thing Megan saw was her little sister having an endotracheal tube being forced down her throat and a paramedic pushing air into her lungs, breathing for her. We found out weeks later through a friend of a friend that one of the paramedics attending Maggie in the helicopter said that he did not believe she would even survive the trip to the hospital.

The drive to University Hospital in San Antonio would be worse than we expected. There were two major accidents on Interstate 10 we had to drive past on our way. Not only were we living our own nightmare, we also saw others in the midst of theirs. I sang, "You are good, your love lasts forever, we will rest in your unfailing love, consume our praise with fire down from heaven and fill our lives with power from above." I sang nonstop, contemplating each word and nuance trying to figure out what the Lord was saying in this. Was it that He was good "no matter what," or the fact that His love lasts forever "no matter what," or that I should praise Him "no matter what"? I noticed my son watching me as he prayed. I had to keep it together for him and my wife. But on the inside, I was screaming. *Oh Lord, please! No! Don't let this be a "no matter what" situation!*

Arriving at a big city hospital on the evening of a major holiday weekend is always a bad scene. It was standing room only in the E.R. as we arrived. Making our way to the reception desk we were told they had a small waiting room for us and someone would meet with us there in a few minutes. I felt like throwing up. All these people were seated in this large waiting room, and they had a special room for us. *What did that mean? Was my imagination running wild again? What had happened in the last hour since we left the scene of the accident, which seemed like an eternity? Was our daughter alive? If so, would she live? How bad were her injuries? Was she disfigured?* A hundred other questions all parents ask themselves but don't have answers to raced through my mind.

The little room quickly filled up with family and friends who had driven to the hospital to be with us and to pray. The room was right next to the door that led to the emergency room. Every time the E.R. door would open, Michelle would start through it, and every time the medical staff would ask her to please stay in the waiting area. "Mr. and Mrs. Faust, we are assessing Maggie to see what we are dealing with," they told us. *She was alive, and they were checking her out! That was something, but we need to see her!* As soon as possible they would let Michelle and I go back one at a time. I thought to myself, *nice try, let's see how that works, because I knew there was not a force on earth that was able to keep Michelle from Maggie much longer.* I had been healed of my former insane protectiveness, but I was still me and I was going through that door, too. After all, my internal clock started ticking when I left the scene of the accident and when we got to the hospital, I knew I would see her. No matter what! Period.

Finally the door opened, and a nurse said one of us could go back to be with her, so Michelle and I went back together. Upon entering the emergency area with all the sterile sights and smells, the technical side of this situation began to unfold. Maggie was in a large room that was very warm, apparently to keep the severely injured from going into a state of shock. I had to see her, but I almost didn't want to look; I wasn't sure I could take it. She was lying on her back with her hands and feet strapped down. Some of the blood had been cleaned from her face, but her hair was still matted with a lot of slowly drying blood. There was a sizable gash on her lower chin and assorted cuts, scraps and bruising on her hands and feet. Of course, that's all I could see since the rest of her body was covered.

After a long while, probably too long, I went back to update our other children on the little we knew because by that point, the main focus was getting her stable so cat scan, x-rays and M.R.I.s would even be possible. As I made my way to the waiting area and through the doors, I noticed many familiar faces. Megan, had taken an informal head count and said that over eighty-five members of our friends and family were at the hospital to support us, and most were still there. Their love and support was amazing.

As Hannah touched down in Nashville, she

immediately turned her cell phone on and by the time she entered the airport terminal she had service. But before she could place a call, her phone began downloading text messages. The first one she opened was from someone she hadn't even spoken to in several months. It read, "So sorry to hear about your little sister, we are praying for your family." Hannah collapsed and wept believing Maggie had died. Immediately her phone rang, and it was Megan with the correct update. She was emotionally spent but relieved.

Sometime in the early morning hours, they felt Maggie was stable enough to perform the necessary CAT scan, x-rays and M.R.I.s to access the extent of her injuries. We were moved to a "hell on earth" called pediatric ICU. If there is a more horrible place to be than pediatric ICU, I'm not aware of where it could be. Every patient is a child in need of intensive care, many whose very life hangs in the balance, not to mention all the gutted parents pacing back and forth. Michelle prayed, and I sang the song over Maggie all night long. By morning it was very obvious to me that if the Lord had given His children an inner thermometer to determine the spiritual temperature of a place or an event, then He had also given us a thermostat to change the temperature of a place or event. The horrible room our daughter lay in transformed and had a peaceful feeling to it. I know, I know we don't live by feelings, blah, blah, blah... you know what I mean. It was real, and I could feel it.

Sometime in the middle of the night two things happened. First, the Lord gave me a revelation about the song. It wasn't so much about His goodness, or His love or even about praise and worship, it was about rest. You are good, and your love lasts forever, we will REST in your unfailing love, consume our praise with fire down from heaven and fill our lives with power from above. You see, we needed what we could not get on our own - rest. The ability, no, the willingness to *not* be in control, to just lose "IT", control that is. In contrast, when Michelle was bleeding to death in the hospital after her surgery, I was taught to stand and to speak life, to fight like a son. With Maggie, I was to rest as a bride of Christ, letting Him have my faith through rest and watch Him just be Himself in our lives.

The other thing I noticed was that I had hardly shed a tear. But now I wept! I went to the hallway outside the ICU and cried my eyes out. Michelle had cried until Maggie was stable, and now our roles reversed. A note to all the husbands out there reading this, if you're doing this thing called marriage right, then you know God has given you a wife that is just as strong as you are, just in different ways. My encouragement to you is, let it be different and cherish it with all your heart.

University Hospital is a teaching hospital and has a very good reputation. I can vouch for their ICU team; they are excellent. I don't remember asking God for patience, but I must have in a moment of weakness because we became very anxious waiting for the results of their tests. Waiting is not something any parent with a child in ICU is ever good at. However, the results finally came, and we began to see what God had been up to.

The first doctor and his team arrived mid-morning, and the conversation went something like this. "Hello, Mr. and Mrs. Faust, My name is Dr. So and So. I have part of the results I'm sure you have been waiting for. It seems Maggie has a broken collar bone, but the good news is we don't have to operate or even put pins it. We don't even have to set it." An hour or two went by, and another team arrived and said, "Hello, Mr. and Mrs. Faust, My name is Dr. Bla Bla Bla and I have part of the results of our testing concerning Maggie. It appears that she has two, maybe three broken ribs, and we're watching her right lung. We don't believe it was damaged badly, probably just bruised, but there is good news concerning her ribs, there is no surgery needed, we don't even have to set them." The next team arrived a few minutes later and informed us she had two fractures to her skull, one in the front left part of her skull and one in the back right part of her skull, and she also had a broken jaw in three places. The metal permanent retainer that was placed in her mouth after her braces were removed by her orthodontist was also broken in half. She would probably lose some teeth, probably two or three. She had a wide gap right in the middle of her bottom row of teeth. They opted not to wire her jaws shut because head trauma patients tend to vomit. They said they wanted to place a large headgear on her in lieu of wiring. But at that point, they weren't too alarmed because it appeared there was no severe swelling of the brain, so surgery to relieve pressure may not be needed. There were two brain bleeds and severe bruising of the brain, but they would wait and see. The next team came in and told us that she had a broken glenoid bone in her left shoulder joint, and she had also broken both scapulas right down the middle. But the good news was they didn't believe surgery was needed to pin them. As a matter of fact, they didn't even need to set them. I started to see a pattern in all this mess. Every team said the same words - not one bone needed surgery and didn't even need to be set.

Let me recap all of this, Maggie had received four stitches in her chin the night before, and they found she not only had many cuts and deep scrapes from the asphalt, but had broken eleven bones. However, not a single one would need surgery to pin it back together and not one would even need setting. Wow! We were far from being out of the woods, but this had to be God at work.

The ICU unit had four hallways that surrounded it, forming a big square; which is where I spent much of my time, and singing under my breath. It began to take on a Jericho feel. To tell you the truth, I don't know if it was something like that in the spirit or if I was just spiritualizing everything in the hopes it would work somehow. So I just walked and sang anyway. It became a waiting game. Wait and see was all they could tell us. They were able to gently bend her broken permanent retainer behind her lower row of teeth so it wouldn't cut the bottom of her tongue.

Maggie woke up off and on and was able to

begin answering some questions the best she could. This sounded very premature given the situation, but it was done to form a base line, neurologically. They would ask a series of questions so later when they asked the same questions, they could compare her answers to help assess her brain function. She slept most of the time. As she slept, one of the nurses helped Michelle gently clean her hair of the debris from the accident. Maggie has hair like a lion's mane, so this was a daunting task Michelle seemed to love. Dirt and gravel, small cedar and oak branches, there was even an earring embedded in her tangles and she wasn't even wearing earrings at the time of the accident. They must have just been part of the junk teenagers keep in their vehicles and were flying around as they flipped. This process took well over an hour to complete. The embedded asphalt and gravel in her scalp would have to wait.

The staff could see Michelle and I were hanging on by a thread, and they showed us a room for parents only with about ten or twelve plastic cots. It wasn't much, but it was a place to lie down for a while. They asked that we keep the lights off at all times because you never knew when another parent would be there trying to sleep, if that were even possible. This would not work for Michelle; she wasn't leaving Maggie, so they brought in a cot for her into Maggie's room. I couldn't hold my eyes open any longer, so I went to the parents' room to try and sleep for a while. I opened the door slowly not to wake anyone who might be inside. I could barely see by the light coming under the door from the hallway. As I laid there, the question of whether or not someone was there in the dark was answered when I began to hear someone crying quietly. It broke my heart. I wanted to say, *let it out. Scream if you want to. It's O.K. I don't mind, I understand. Let it all out.* But instead, I just lay there and whispered the song under my breath and prayed. I never got any sleep, but I don't think I was there to sleep. Later I met the person who was weeping. He was the father of a little girl that while on vacation swam down to the bottom of his brother in law's pool and got her finger stuck in the drain. I was able to pray for him and his wife later that day. The next morning they were gone. I don't know what happened, but I still pray for them from time to time. Praying for them felt so good, I could see it in their eyes; it was like water to their soul. They were from Boston with no friends and little family in San Antonio, and I had more friends, family and support than I needed.

Soon thereafter I went by the ICU waiting area and I saw an older lady from our church just sitting there praying for us. We didn't even know she had been there, so I went to her with an update on Maggie. She could see my exhaustion and asked if I was able to get any sleep. I said "no", but that reminded me to tell her to pray for the couple who I had just prayed for. She said, "I'm proud of you, you just be a light in a dark place." For the life of me, I don't know why I said what I said next. I will just blame it on a lack of sleep. I looked at her and replied, "I'm going to be the black plague on the devil's ass while I'm here." She looked back at me, a little shocked, but she completely understood what I meant, and just smiled and hugged me. But from that point on, I began to give what I had been given. I prayed for just about anybody who would let me, in the ICU, cafeteria, hallways, patients and nurses alike, it didn't matter. As they say in the old war movies, this was a target rich environment.

The third day they moved Maggie into a private room right across the hall from the main ICU unit. She was allowed to have a few visitors at a time, which made her siblings very happy. We were able to take them into ICU one at a time, but only for a few minutes each. This room wasn't as scary looking as ICU, and we could be together much of the time. The hospital staff and the different teams were amazed at her progress, including the neurosurgeon. His staff had been in several more times to work with Maggie and seemed to be pleased with her progress, but there was no way to pin down the neurology team for definitive answers. So much about the brain is unknown and it would just take time to see how things developed or didn't develop. As a matter of fact the head neurosurgeon, (I can't recall his name so I will refer to him as Dr. Know-It-All) wanted to run more tests and MRIs. Please understand, I'm not being derogatory about him because he really did seem to know it all. So, more waiting.

One of the hardest things to deal with was her upper back. There were very deep scrapes over the breaks of her scapulas that had to be cleaned and dressed regularly. We were informed later that less than 1% of all breaks or fractures involve a scapula because your shoulder blades are flat and very well protected by an intricate series of muscles and tendons. Breaking a scapula in conjunction with a glenoid bone almost always requires surgery. Maggie had broken both of her scapulas and a glenoid bone, which at this point wouldn't require surgery.

The results of more tests came in, and all of her injuries looked surprisingly good. It was very obvious the nursing staff and different teams of physicians were also surprised with the entire situation. The tone in their voices and their demeanor gave us a lot of relief. We began to tell them why and testify about our Lord and faith in Him. On several occasions, we prayed for the staff about issues they were dealing with in their lives. It was God, and it was awesome to see Him use us in the midst of all we were living through.

There was talk of releasing her the following afternoon. It was surreal. We had only been in the hospital for four and a half days at that point. Then Dr. Know-It-All ordered another MRI. What was going on? Was he just being thorough or was something wrong?

We were on the verge of being released, and it would just be a matter of time to allow the bones to heal. Most of the teams said some rehab would be required. Some suspected a lot, while others were more optimistic. We had also been given some training from the Neuro team about the mental exercises they wanted us to perform at home. They also gave us the name of a Neurotherapist in our area. They said it was very common for head trauma patients not to remember anything from the day of the accident, and they would be surprised if she remembered anything from a few days before the accident to several days after the accident. It would also not be alarming if she didn't remember casual acquaintances and even distant relatives, but if she didn't remember close friends, relatives, family pets, etc., they would need to be informed immediately.

We were okayed to be released, so we assumed all was well with the last MRI, and that Dr. Know-It-All would meet with us before we left the hospital. We also assumed he would give us some last minute instructions and make sure we understood the procedures we needed to perform at home. This would not be the case.

We were taken in to a separate room to meet with him. It was here he would stab us through the heart with information we could not possibly have anticipated. He said that what he had to tell us was going to sound unreasonable, but it was somewhat common for them to find something totally unrelated while working with a patient. It's called an incidental finding. Our hearts sank. What the hell was he talking about? This was crazy! We were almost out the door!

He said that the reason for the last MRI was to get a different angle on a spot on her spinal cord that looked abnormal on the first MRI. The last MRI had shown a place on her spine that could be something very serious. He said it could only be caused by one of three things and that one of those could be definitely ruled out. The first would be the result of a very specific birth defect, which we knew she did not have. The second would be the result of a crushed spine when she obviously didn't have either. The third thing that could cause this was a tumor. He said they would do another MRI in a few months to see if the spot on her spine had changed or grown. He encouraged us not to Google it because it would only distress us. Ha! That's a laugh, distress us! Wow! The English language is so totally bankrupt when trying to describe how parents feel in moments like these. We felt the same feelings and emotions we did at the scene of the accident, only this time we were completely exhausted. The other problem was that it would take another MRI to determine its growth, but because tumors of the spine are typically very slow growing, another MRI could not be done for several months. Months!? Are you kidding me?

He tried to encourage us, seeing the panic in our eyes. He left us there to be alone for a while. We held each other and prayed through our tears. We would stand on the fact that God had done amazing things so far, and He was not a God of half measures.

We didn't tell anyone about this except a few close friends so they could agree with us in prayer. We had rationalized God knew about all of these things before we did, but I didn't want anyone to know about these developments. Maybe I didn't want to try and explain something that I didn't even understand myself, or maybe I didn't want all of the small talk going around about the poor Faust family. I wanted instead for people to stand with us on the fact she was alive, and God's hand was on her. Basically, all I knew to do was... You are good, your love lasts forever, we will

REST in your unfailing love, consume our praise with fire down from heaven and fill our lives with power from above.

I made the trip back to our car dealership to get a minivan. I removed the rear seat and placed a twin size mattress in its place. A close friend of mine was delivering a hospital bed to our house to replace Maggie's bed.

The trip home with Maggie made me a nervous wreck, talk about defensive driving. We made the trip in just over an hour. We were relieved to get Maggie into her temporary bed and see her comfortable.

The choices were simple, as are many things with God. We would learn that rest is a weapon or we would struggle. That is not to say that resting in the unfailing love of God is always easy, but it is always right. I am a firm believer in our need to lose "IT" in order to do this - to embrace our position as a bride of Christ and let Him be for us what we cannot and should not be for ourselves. Sometimes we are to step into our identity as sons and daughters of God conquering the enemy on the battlefield of life, other times we are to step back into the Lord as His bride and let Him protect us and save us. It is in deep intimacy we learn the difference. Just because the enemy rattles his saber on the battlefield does not mean we are called to fight; it may be that we are instead called to rest. We fight when the Lord says, not when the enemy says, because we are to be led by the Spirit and not by our own good intent.

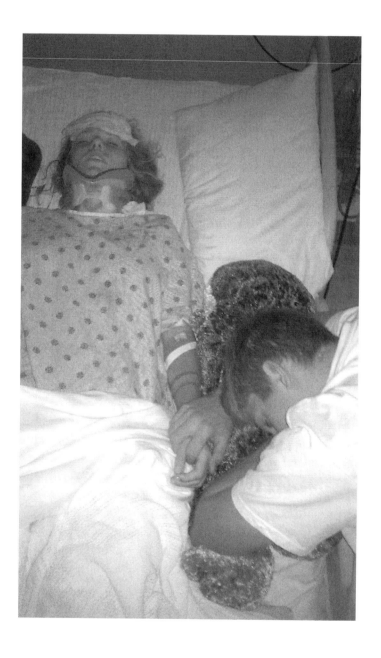

"You prepare a table for me in the presence of my enemies. You anoint my head with oil, my cup overflows." ~**Psalm 23:5**

Can you imagine that? The Lord of all, the God of the entire universe and universes prepares a banquet for you and makes YOUR enemy watch! Then He hangs a banner of love over you. Close your eyes and open your heart, right now. See it in your mind's eye. I dare you! Does that banner look like Him sacrificing Himself on the cross so that He could serve you a feast that will sustain you for eternity?

IF you are reading this right now and you don't know Him, or you are a half-way (luke warm) Christian, please brother or sister, don't continue to walk in deception. That's Christian-ese for please don't continue to be stupid. When I wrote about my past and who I was and how I was living, I lied when I said I wasn't going to candy coat it. I did. Sorry! (But after all, I did say that I was just going to hit the highlights). This relationship with Him, the one He is relentlessly seeking with you, not the one you are considering with Him, but one you choose to agree with, is so simple. It's like everything else with this unreasonable, maniac lover of your soul. Just say, "Lord, if you're real, make yourself real to me!"

Keep reading; I have something else to say to you later. Don't worry it's not doom and gloom. I don't do gloom and doom, I was taught better than that, because it's the goodness of God that drives men to repentance. The Lord prepares a table for you... think about that as you read...

> *"And when he had given thanks he broke the bread*
> *and said this is my body which is for YOU, do this*
> *in remembrance of me, in the same way after supper*
> *he took the cup of wine saying, this cup is the new*
> *covenant in my blood, do this whenever you drink it*
> *in remembrance of me."*
> **~1Corinthians 11:24-30** (Emphasis mine.)

Wow! What a table He has prepared for our lives, now, and in the eternity that is coming! Can you imagine what's on the menu?

Everything was going as well as can be expected. Maggie was awake much more often and was communicating well. We were hypersensitive concerning her brain function. We began to notice as we monitored her food and liquid intake that she was taking in a lot of water, an abnormal amount. This could be a sign of pituitary gland damage, and if it continued we would have to make the trip back to San Antonio within a few hours. The pituitary gland is about the size of a pea weighing 0.5 grams. It is not part of the brain, but a protrusion off the bottom of the hypothalamus at the base of the brain and rests in a small, bony cavity covered by a dural fold (diaphragma sellae) situated in the sphenoid bone in the middle cranial fossa at the base of the brain. All that to say it's not easy to damage, and it is a very important gland that controls a lot of stuff, and she sure didn't need to be dealing with something else right now. I had seen God do amazing things, things with which no one could argue. Maggie had been in an accident that had almost a zero chance of survival, she had eleven broken bones that didn't even need to be set or have surgery or pins, she was home in just a few days after being admitted into PICU, and all of the trench warriors (PICU nurses) told us how amazed they were with her, and how and I quote "lucky she was". I have to mention their willingness to be corrected by a crazy Christian father who said luck had nothing to do with it, and who would begin to cry and try to pray for them at the drop of a hat. Who does that sound like to you? And they weren't even trying to avoid me. I love Richard, he had taught me well! We called our friends and family to pray for her, especially Richard and Glenda, and after seeing all that God had done so far, it was like calling in a spiritual airstrike. The next morning the symptoms were gone, completely. Yea God!!

Back to our private waiting game.

We had an appointment at University Hospital a few days later for more x-rays, etc. to make sure none of her eleven broken bones had shifted or needed any attention. I was dreading this appointment for Maggie because even though she was feeling oddly good, the trip would be difficult given all of her broken bones. But as I thought to myself, something didn't sound right. Why did I think it would be uncomfortable for her? I didn't think she would enjoy the trip, but after all, she wasn't even taking pain killers anymore. She hadn't even complained recently. Was it because it would hurt her to make the trip or that privately I didn't want to hear any more crap about more issues she might have? I secretly thought, *what if they look at her spine?* I was sure they would given the fact that most of the damage was in close proximity to that area. I just didn't want to hear about it. I mean, if we needed to know something then let's get it on, but if we were going to leave the hospital being sucked back into the void of this nightmarish waiting game, I just didn't think that I could take it.

Like most men, we don't want to hear about problems we can't kill. It's not that we want to avoid issues, ladies, but contrary to popular belief, we are created to attack them and anything that threatens our loved ones. This, ladies, has been a source of contention since the world began. "He's just not sensitive to me," you may say and maybe he isn't, but that's a different issue. When it comes to you or his children or issues concerning the wellbeing of his family, men want and need an enemy to kill, not one to talk to or rationalize with or figure a way around to make things better through negotiation and crying, but kill. Ladies if you find this quality in your man, cherish, celebrate and cultivate it. The world needs more men that think this way, even if they're a little misdirected at times.

Women need patience, too. What would happen if more fathers and husbands felt this way, even if their wives didn't recognize it as the treasure it is right away? Speaking of the other issue for a minute, guys, be more sensitive to your wives, especially when things are tough. Picture in your minds that stress is a monster and is trying to hurt your wife, and you must KILL it! But the only weapon you have is called... Wait for it, wait for it... Sensitivity. Yes, that's right gentlemen, sensitivity! It's like Kryptonite to the stress your wife is feeling. And you have the opportunity to rub it onto her wounds like a sensuous ointment to her soul, unlocking her innermost feelings and desires. How's that for a paradigm shift, boys? Nothing like a little perspective to get you back on track. YOU'RE WELCOME LADIES!

Maggie has a lot of friends, and we have a large part of our family that lives in the area. After she got home from the hospital, it seemed the doorbell was always ringing. She was doing great and had very little pain. As a matter of fact, Maggie only took pain pills for two days after she was home because she said they made her sleepy, and she had slept enough. Maggie has always been very active. She loves sports and working out and evidently driving too fast on the "FUN" country roads. As far as we could tell, she didn't remember anything from the day of the accident, very little of her hospital stay and not much of the ride home.

One afternoon Megan was sitting with her in her room and Maggie asked, "Who was that guy?" Megan replied, "Which guy?" Maggie said, "That tall guy that just left a few minutes ago?" Megan was confused because there was no one who matched that description that had been there. Maggie had heard us talking about how she might not remember casual acquaintances or distant relatives, so we thought she was possibly a little embarrassed that she didn't recognize him. Frustrated, she pressed Megan by insisting that he had just been there earlier, and she had seen him at the hospital and at the accident, but couldn't remember his name. She thought it would become obvious to him that she didn't remember his name and hurt his feelings. Megan knew that Maggie hadn't remembered anything so far about the day of the accident, and probably never would, or even much of her hospital stay, so she chose to ask Maggie what he looked like instead of arguing the point that no one like that had been there. Maggie described him as someone who kind of dressed like a dork because he wore hiking boots with his socks pulled half way to his knees and wore navy blue cargo shorts. He had blonde hair and she also said he was tall like a basketball player.

Megan told Maggie that didn't describe anyone she knew. A number of her friends had been there earlier that afternoon, but two things were obvious to Megan, none were tall, and more importantly all of them had been girls. Maggie kept insisting that Megan wasn't in the room when he was there, or that she just didn't notice him. To that Megan replied, "How could I not notice him when I haven't left your room?" They both realized what Maggie was describing at about the same time. She could only be seeing an angel. As she reflected on this Maggie said she could remember lying on the ground at the accident, and when she opened her eyes her head was turned to one side and she could see a pair of shoes. As she looked up she saw blue cargo shorts and a person kneeling down smiling at her. She had a sensation like she was floating. She remembered closing her eyes, and he was gone, but everything looked like it had a yellowish gold hue, and she felt like she was still floating. Then she noticed him again, but this time as she lay there he just smiled and walked by her. Later she said he was in her hospital room with her, just smiling at her. After they had visited in her room at home, she couldn't recall what was said after he left. Everyone was so excited about Maggie's angel when they heard about it, but strangely, Michelle and I weren't too surprised after all God had done. *Why not? We thought, that sounded like God.* Nothing seemed off His menu, even a super tall blonde angel with bad fashion sense, according to a sixteen year old.

So the day of her first checkup has arrived; it had been thirteen days since the accident. Her appointment was early, so that meant we had to get up very early to make the 70 mile trip back to University Hospital in San Antonio. There were more MRIs and x-rays, and then a nurse led us to an examination room. Tick-tock, tick-tock more waiting. As the minutes passed, I began to get anxious. This was taking a long time and not just because I was an impatient father. Forty-five minutes had gone by. *What had they found? Why was this taking so long?*

The door to our little exam room opened. A doctor we had never seen before stepped in, and immediately put his hand up in front of him as if to say, I know you've been waiting a long time, but it couldn't be helped. *Oh crap, here it comes,* I thought to myself. *They had found something else and needed a second opinion, that's why it took so long.* But then he said, "Everything looks great; in fact I had to request her original x-ray from the day of her accident to compare them to today's because I couldn't find the breaks! It looks like she is healing fine, I could just barely see the shadows of where the breaks were." He then moved on and said, "I see here in your file you're involved in sports at school. I'm going to write you a note because I don't want you to push it too hard, I tend to err on the side of caution."

I'm sure the looks on our faces confused him a bit as I asked, "What did you say? " He then started over about preferring to be cautious. I said quickly, "No, what did you say about her breaks?" The doctor said again, "Everything looks great and what took so long is we were comparing the pictures from today with the originals. " I then asked him if he realized that the accident had only been thirteen days ago. Looking down at the files in his hands, he simply said, "NO." To which I said, "Is that normal?" Again with a very confused look on his face he simply said, "No," still looking at the files in his hands. I am a car dealer, which means I am not usually at a loss for words, but at that moment all I could get out was "Speak more words," to which he quickly snapped back into doctor mode, a little offended and more perplexed than anything, he said it wasn't his job to inhibit people from going on with their everyday lives, that his job was to read the results and give an opinion, and he could only report the results he had found. He then said he was releasing her, but we needed to have her cleared for sports with the Neurology Department as well. We were so dumbfounded that we really didn't notice when he left the room.

We left that department and headed for another to have a different x-ray done of her head to see how the skull fractures and jaw were faring. This went just about the same way with less fanfare, probably because we were in a little bit of shock about what we had just learned. They said the skull looked great, and it appeared she was not going to lose any teeth because the break was now healed and it didn't go through the root of the teeth as the original x-ray had shown. You know, the three breaks in her jaw, the one that was so severe that it broke the metal permanent retainer right in the middle? The broken retainer would need to be replaced, and she still had a pretty wide gap in her bottom row of teeth, which we didn't understand but who cared, what a wonderful report we had! Yea God! The drive home was awesomely strange. God had healed her - eleven broken bones in an instant, home in just a few days, hardly any pain meds, and now doctors and x-rays can't even find the breaks after only thirteen days, which should normally take six or seven weeks to heal. On top of that, she was released to play sports. Really!? Are you kidding me? God is awesome!

During the drive home, Michelle and I were thinking the same thing. If God had done all of this, what about the other issue that the head neurologist had spoken about? We didn't speak openly about it because Maggie was with us in the car, and we hadn't mentioned it to her at that point. She had enough to deal with. We just reveled in what God had done and spent the time using our cell phones to call anyone and everyone we knew to tell of what God had done.

It would still be several more weeks before we would be able to make an appointment with her orthodontist. When a person breaks their jaw, an orthodontist typically won't see you until the jaw has had time to heal completely, which is between six and seven weeks. This is because they have to put your jaw under some pressure to replace the retainer and this obviously can't be done until the 'lawyers' say so and the bone has completely healed. So you know what was next... more waiting.

But so what! This was just too awesome. Over the next few weeks, we would tell anyone and everyone who would listen what God had done. I would even brag about how God had completely healed my daughter, and the only thing I would have to do was have her permanent retainer fixed. You know, the only man-made item on her entire body.

After a few days of enjoying the fact that we had a proof positive miracle or miracles, reality began to creep back in that we were still dealing with a life and death situation concerning her spinal cord. We had good days and bad days while walking through this valley. You gotta hand it to the enemy sometimes, he really is good at his job. He is an Olympic gold medalist liar. I guess it makes sense in some ways since that's the only real weapon he has.

*"And having disarmed the powers and authorities, he made a public spectacle of them, triumphing over them by the cross." ~***Colossians 2:15**

Other translations replace the word 'disarmed' with 'stripped' and the word 'spectacle' with 'shame'. So I ask you, with that scripture in mind, what weaponry does the enemy still possess? I mean really, we're talking about Satan here, the dark one, Beelzebub himself. Surely this scripture must be a metaphor scripturally because we all know that Satan has great power, right? We can't just fear him for no reason. We live here on this earth, in the here and the now, and we see all the havoc the enemy wreaks on the earth. So what power do YOU say he has? If you just answered that question in any way, then you are willing to write off this truth as part of your life. Ouch! I know it hurts a little for me to say it that way, but it won't hurt as much as your choice to believe that the enemy has power, and what's more, the scripture you just read has no truth to you. We can't have it both ways. Either you choose to believe what the Word says, or you don't, and contrary to popular belief, you don't have to have it proven to you. You must believe it, by faith in the One who can't lie to you.

Here's the problem, we see and live in this fallen world and see the enemy plague people's lives, and sadly our own, and we give him credit for having all manner of power. But scripture is the baseline of the truth. The truth is, the enemy gets a lot of credit for the things we experience in this fallen world, coupled with the sad fact that scripture also says in Jeremiah 17 that

"the, heart of man is wicked above all things, who can know it." ~**Jeremiah 17:9**

Many, many, many, many times when I have sinned, the enemy and his minions weren't even in the same county when I chose to sin, whatever it was. What do you think the Lord of All meant when He inspired the words in Colossians 2 when He wrote the words:

"disarmed/stripped and made a spectacle/shamed the enemy"? ~**Colossians 2:15**

I don't know about you, but I'm a simple Texas redneck, and I think He meant what He said. After all, the Bible calls us sheep and in my experience sheep are stupid, so He didn't make it complicated. It's said that sheep are so stupid, they're born lookin' for a place to die. Hmmmm...? Which means they'll die for almost any reason... Hmmmm...? Wasn't Jesus called the Lamb of God? Bigger HMMMM...?

He came here, and He went to the cross for any and all reasons man could think of. Our sin put Him there. It was an act of his very, very free will to carry the cross that he knew he would be nailed to. He carried it up that hill that day thinking about you and me. It was there that the richest person of all, chose to give his perfect life in the most horrible of ways, and worse still, be separated from God His Father even for a second. It is almost unfathomable. But for love for you and me, there was no way Jesus wouldn't have done it. It really is a crazy love. I can't tell you how many times that I have told Him how crazy He is for loving me. He just says, "call me what you will. I adore you." Then He trumps my brazen statement by saying, "Troy, you do know that you are my favorite, don't you?" I only wish that I still had the ability to blush in the spirit. But, that's a completely different book. I've said this to many people over the years in the course of discussion and counseling. Some of them get this look on their faces like, "Oh no! Did you hear what he just said? He just called God crazy. Oh Man! He's in trouble", or "How disrespectful" or something like that.

I have always thought my sin that put Him there with nails in His hands and feet, with a crown of thorns on His head might be just a little more offensive than my verbiage about His love. I really believe He's not offended by my quips, which help me begin to understand His ridiculous love for me. We need to be real, and by real, I mean really real with Him. Anything else is offensive, and I mean really offensive. He's looking for intimacy with me, and not my attempt to be you or someone else I think has it all together. Or even your version of how I should express my being overwhelmed by His love in words. The best of me has to be me, the real me, or it's a fake impersonator, a poser. Believe me He will know the difference, the question is will you? You may settle it within yourself that you have been real with God even at a deep, intimate level that you are comfortable with, but He will not settle until He has all of you. He is relentless.

Let's get back to the subject of the devil. After all, we are taught to study the ways of our enemy; here's the real truth. The enemy has no power except the power of a lie. If you believe them, they have power. If you don't, they have no power. He is called the great deceiver for a reason. If I tell you a lie and you CHOOSE to believe me, then you have given me power over your thoughts. In contrast, if I lie to you and you choose not to believe me, then I have no power over you. Simple isn't it. His big, huge, ugly, scary plan is just that simple. Think about it, do you think the enemy would do anything else? Do you think he's capable of an original thought that didn't originate in the mind of God. Of course not. He always counterfeits everything the Lord does. So if it's important to understand it's not good enough to believe IN God, but we must also BELIEVE God, then it's also important to stop believing in the power of the enemy and start believing he has been stripped bare at the cross. He only possesses the power of a lie. According to Colossians 2:15 you get to determine its power over you, or lack thereof, not him.

Here's my best advice, every time the enemy attacks you with lies, remind him of his future, in contrast to yours. Don't treat him like a hot potato and say what I used to. Say, "Get away from me in Jesus name, I rebuke you, in Jesus name, I claim the blood of Jesus over my life, flee from me you unclean spirit." I love to say, "Satan before I let you leave, let me ask you a simple question. How hot do you think hell is going to be? And just how long is eternity? The same person that made heaven so crazy awesome for me, He took that same passion and energy and made a place so heinous and horrible, just for you, the hater of His bride." You will notice the enemy hates to be reminded of his future, and he will be gone. You most likely won't get the chance to add all those other Christian-ese verbs and adjectives, use them if you want to, but He only recognizes your recognition of truth and intimacy with God. Now if you wanna talk about fleeing! That will rewrite his definition for him.

"Resist the enemy and he will flee from you".
~James 4:7

We talk about quenching the fiery darts of the enemy almost every time we pray for someone. I say it's time we shoot a few of our own. Keep it simple. He fashions darts to shoot at you, so fashion some of your own. Not somebody else's weaponry, but some of your own. Think about it this way, if he's close enough to spit on your brain, then you're close enough to spit on his. I am convinced that it's high time he was afraid, and it will happen when you stand up with sword in hand and proclaim truth over his existence and yours. Truth always wins! I didn't say it, you didn't say it, but God said it. Please don't take me wrong here, I'm not advocating that you run out on the battlefield every time the enemy raises his ugly head. We should always step back into our intimacy with the Lord and see what He says about it. Find out what His plans are for you in this or that situation. Sometimes the Lord prepares a banquet table for you in the presence of your enemies, sometimes, it's a set-up of the enemy to steal your rest, but sometimes the Lord equips us and shoots us from His bow into the battle. But always keep in mind, confidence in the outcome of the battle doesn't come from your abilities, but your orders. The battle is for the mind... so be what you were called to be... choose to be MORE than a conqueror. Conquerors of old didn't take many prisoners.

There we were, standing and believing God was not a God of half measures, but yet on some days still fearing the worst. This was a process of learning to stand together, taking every thought captive, applying scripture to every thought like it had the ability to take us off track and derail us. At other times, thoughts would come through our minds that were laced with joy, peace and conviction to strengthen our resolve. We learned a huge lesson in those days, like it's just as important to agree viciously with the truth as it is to disagree viciously with the lies. King David said, "Oh Lord, let me love what you love and let me hate what you hate." Sounds like, oh Lord, help me believe You and not just in You, doesn't it? King David had ownership of the truths he was writing. The question is, do we?

CHAPTER 16

God Just Showing Off!

being confident of this, that he who began a good work in you will carry it on to completion until the day of Christ Jesus. ~**Philippians 1:6**

So back to Maggie's story. However, first I need to remind you that at the beginning of this book I told you there were things that were going to be hard to believe for some of you. I said some of you were absolutely going to love it and rejoice with us in it, and some of you would struggle to understand it, but would agree God can do anything He wants, and others would just find it all too hard to believe. To tell you the truth, what I'm about to write shook me at the time. I don't know why. After all, He can do whatever He wants to, but I hadn't even prayed for what happened next, not that I didn't think He could do it, but I guess I hadn't let my mind run wild enough with the possibilities. Makes me wonder what other things I've missed along the way.

Time had passed, and Maggie was doing great. She was a walking, talking testimony. In some ways, it was as if there had never been an accident, other than the fact that there was no way any of us could ever forget what God had done. It had been almost six weeks since the accident, which meant enough time had passed and we could make an appointment with her orthodontist to repair her permanent retainer. We were going into a weekend, so we decided we would make the appointment for the following Monday. She hadn't complained much about it during the whole ordeal, and she hadn't mentioned much about it. In fact; we had to remind ourselves to make the appointment.

I decided to buy dinner for our family from our favorite Mexican restaurant that night. Maggie went with me, and she drove. We arrived and placed our order at the drive thru. Maggie handed them my credit card, and I put our order in the back seat and signed the receipt; Maggie raised her window. Somewhere in the middle of this very simple transaction, Maggie simply said, in a very matter of fact way, "Dad, my retainer is fixed." I replied with something like, "Yes, I know honey, we're making you an appointment on Monday." She said, "Dad, my retainer is fixed." My head snapped her direction, and I asked, "WHAT DID YOU SAY? Did you just say that your retainer is healed, I mean fixed?" She nodded her head, yes. I asked, "When? Just now? Open your mouth." She did, but instead reached for the rearview mirror, bending it down to inspect her new or repaired, or replaced retainer...

Are you kidding me?!! I was freaking out. I grabbed her face and directed it towards me so I could inspect for myself. I quickly noticed the gap between her teeth was also gone. Sitting there blocking the drive thru at the restaurant, I wept and thanked this Savior of ours. Through my tears I said to Him, "You're just showin' off now!" Once I was semi composed, I used my cell phone to call Michelle, but when I heard her voice, well, let's just say composure went out the window. She thought something was wrong because she could tell I was crying. I told her that everything was fine, more than fine and to meet us in the driveway. There we wept together thanking God once again for His ridiculous mercy and love for us. That's right sports fans, God had fixed, healed or replaced her metal permanent retainer. To tell you the truth, we don't know which He chose to do, and frankly, we don't care. Remember, I had bragged all over the place that God had completely healed our daughter, and all I had to do was have her retainer replaced, well, as God would have it, we didn't even have to do that.

During this amazing event, I noticed something. Maggie was very thankful and grateful, but she didn't react to this miracle retainer like we did. She seemed oddly content to just accept it with little or no fanfare. As we burned up the airwaves with our cell phones sharing with our friends and family what God had done once again, she just said she wasn't sure when it happened; she just noticed it was fixed, or whatever, and she didn't think it was that big of a deal, especially after all that He had done already. She said. "It's just metal, Dad." Out of the mouths of babes... I was rebuked and corrected by the faith of my daughter. I was marveling in the wrong things. I had become more amazed by His power than His love for me. I had received revelation from the Lord that THE IMPOSSIBLE IS 'NOTHING', but I still hadn't seen the big picture.

> *"For I am convinced that neither death nor life,*
> *neither angels nor demons, neither the present nor*
> *future, nor anything else in all creation, will be able*
> *to separate us from the love of God that is in Christ*
> *Jesus our Lord."* ~**Romans 8:38-39**

Do you see where God put the emphasis? On His love and nothing shares the stage with His love, not even His power.

My ceiling was most definitely my daughter's floor, and even with everything we had been through, I still hadn't seen what she was just able to simply accept. I am forever grateful to see the purity of her receptiveness, and His love and mercy for my family.

Time marches on, and the day of the big exam had arrived. Months had passed since we saw what God had done with her retainer. Our faith had shot up like a rocket, but over the months, we would learn to hold onto what we had been given. The enemy would contend with us for seemingly every inch of ground we had been given or had claimed. Sometimes by fighting, sometimes by just standing and other times by choosing to rest in the middle of the battlefield.

An MRI machine is a creepy space age looking device that looks like it's right out of a George Lucas' Star Wars movie. They provide an amazing service, but when you see your child being slid into one, and all you can do is wait for the results, it just leaves you with an ominous eerie feeling. We prayed together with Maggie, and we would stand and believe together as well. The MRI was complete, and we were reunited with Maggie and were directed to Dr. Know-It-Alls office while he and his staff read the results of the tests.

The good doctor entered and having dealt with many parents waiting for results concerning their children, he wasted no time and quickly said, "Everything looks great. There are no issues to report with her spine and nothing needs attention." Then the questions started to flow from us, but in reality, God was truly not a God of half measures. He in fact, had completely healed our daughter. We asked the doctor if it wasn't a birth defect, and it wasn't a tumor, and if it wasn't caused by the accident, then what was it in the first place? As our questions got more pointed and direct in our excitement, he simply said he had no answers. He said the human body is very complex, and we just don't know everything, and we should just enjoy the fact that this had a happy ending. With that, our conference was over. However, as we were all exiting his office, I asked a question we hadn't thought about in the midst of the nightmare, since it really had no impact at the time. I asked just out of curiosity, where on her spine was this whatever it was had been. He turned Maggie around and pointed to the middle of her back directly between her scapulas. Michelle told me later while the three of us waited in his office for the results, she could feel the presence of the Lord enter the room and then her mother's heart, and she knew all was well. We were going to get another perfect report. A few days later I received this letter in the mail.

John C. Key MD
PRIMARY CARE

Kerrville, Texas   78028

January 10, 2012

Mr. Troy Faust
Kerrville, Texas   78028

Dear Troy:

I know you've already received a lot of well-deserved praise
for your powerful testimony given in church this weekend, so
I'll not just add to that. But I did want to say that my
background made me hear your testimony in a little different
way from most folks.

Before you ever knew me—the years 1976 to 1992—I was a
Board-certified trauma surgeon and had occasion to attend
many folks in a similar mess to Maggie's injury. There are a
couple of things that really strike fear into the heart of a
trauma surgeon when he is called to the ER—among them
are (1) a history of being ejected from the vehicle and (2) a
broken scapula. (One broken scapula will do—you don't
need two). It takes a lot of blunt force to break a scapula,
and when you see one you know that the person's body has
suffered tremendous internal force and major injury to lungs,
heart, brain and abdominal organs is the rule, not the
exception. Usually the recovery time is measured in weeks,
not days... if they are fortunate enough to survive at all. So I
wanted you to know that I had a real first-hand appreciation
for the magnitude of Maggie's Miracle.

Mr. Troy Faust
Page 2 of 2

Second, the point you made about "Believing God: was really convicting to me.   As you started your testimony you made the point about having to handle the dual trips to Costa Rica and Brazil just a few days apart—and you TRUSTED GOD that everything would be OK. I kept that thought in my mind throughout your witness, and was so glad that you ended your testimony with the message that we have to BELIEVE GOD, not just believe IN God.   It is a shortcoming that I have suffered up until now. On the strength of your testimony, Suzanne and I have resolved to start believing and trusting God for his promises. Oh sure, we have always said that we did, but it seems like every time we look for remedies "in the natural" instead of by faith alone.

Troy, I praise God for the richness of His blessings to you in this past year and in the year to come, especially for granting Maggie's Miracle and enabling you and your family to avoid that unbearable loss.

Sincerely,

John C. Key MD

The weight his letter carried started to open my eyes to the depth of what I believed God had done. First, let's take a common sense look at the proximity of the spinal issue in relationship to the other injuries. Get a mental picture of this by imagining Maggie's back. She had a broken collar bone, a broken glenoid bone, broken ribs, a bruised lung, two brain bleeds with two skull fractures, a broken jaw, and last but not least, she had broken both scapulas. Remember, scapulas are some of the most difficult bones to break in the human body because of their protected location and the energy it takes to break one, let alone both of them. The issue on her spine was located directly between both scapulas and centered in the middle of the mass of damage her body had sustained. As I reflected on all of this, the thought occurred to me, *What was the angel doing at the scene of the accident?* I'm not a theologian, but I have never heard nor read about the Lord sending an angel anywhere just to spectate.

We began to hear of the experiences our close friends had while thanking God for Maggie's healing. Things like "as I thanked God, I had a sense that He said to me, that I had no idea the depth of healing," or "I healed her 'all the way'." One of my closest friends who had been at the scene said she died, and God had raised her from the dead on the asphalt that day. We don't know what God did as our baby laid on the asphalt, but we do know it was miraculous.

As we left the hospital, cell phones back in our hands, it wouldn't take long to inform friends and family about this new-found miracle, because we hadn't told many. Those who knew rejoiced and thanked God with us.

The drive home was strange for me. I didn't know how to act. We had thanked God before we even got into our car in the hospital parking garage to drive home. There must be more I should do or say, this just felt odd. If He would have asked me to stop the car and start preaching in the street, I would have done it without hesitation and gladly. Being a missionary to Africa was not off the table. I went through a whole list of things I would gladly do for Him. Then I remembered part of a sermon I had heard when I was just a kid. The preacher whose name I can't recall said, "Many people say that they are willing to do all manner of things for Jesus, even die for him, but Jesus isn't asking, "Who will die for me?" ,but instead, "who is willing to live for me?" There it was again, He was gently reminding me not to confuse what He had called me to do, with who He had called me to be. His focus was, and always had been, to love me, and through His love for me, He would help me step into my identity in Him. It's through understanding my identity that He and I will do great exploits, according to His written and living Word, because He says so.

It's this identity that I would like to address now. The Lord showed me something one day many years ago that has helped me keep my "eye on the ball", so to speak. He revealed to me that I was created to be in intimate relationship with Him, bringing glory and honor to that relationship. By walking in the truth, I could bring God the greatest pleasure He could ever feel; according to scripture no greater joy does the Father have than to see me walking in the truth. The picture in my mind was of a hammer trying to drive a screw and a screw driver attempting to hammer a nail; it just doesn't work because neither was created or fashioned or intended for that purpose. So in my life, and in yours, the easiest thing in the world to do is what you were intended to be. You were created to be in relationship with Him. PERIOD. My best advice for you is to not complicate it. Filter everything in your lives through His crazy love for you.

If you are reading this and you don't know Him or even believe He exists, then I only have one thing to say to you. Whether you want to believe me or the things you've read is completely irrelevant to your life and future. But, whether or not you believe the Lord who chose you, loves you, died for you and lives for you, and currently adores you right where you are right now, does have a huge impact on your forever.

So I have a very simple suggestion for you. And no, I'm not going to ask you to read the sinners prayer, or try to convert you in any way. The sad truth is, some of you will choose not to believe, even though He said His heart is that none would perish, but all should come to the saving knowledge of what He has done for us and is doing for us. I am just going to dare you to say to the Lord, "If you are real and you really do love me, then please make yourself real to me." Open your heart and mind, and I believe you will see the truth of His love for you. I am convinced He loves you so much He just can't help himself. It's not that He will do anything for your love, but rather He has already done everything for your love. For God so loved the world that He gave, He didn't take a thing, except our sin upon Himself. Remember, He is the same yesterday, today and forever, and He's going to have His original intention. PERIOD. Question is? Are YOU going to choose to agree with Him? Or not...?..

WHAT IF?

What if it's all true? What if His intentions for you are better than you ever thought? What if His heart for you is bigger than you've ever dreamed?

What if you believed Him, not just in Him? What if He really means what He says about having plans for you? Good plans, plans to give you a hope and a future, plans to prosper you mentally, physically, emotionally, financially, spiritually and even sexually. The Word (written and living) gives us insight about how He feels about blessing and prospering His children.

"pressed down, shaken together and running over,"
~Luke 6:38

I know Him as the God of more than enough, not the God of just enough. The truth is... IT'S TRUE! He has such an excessive personality! I love it!

What's my part in all of this, you ask. Well, I'm glad you asked, so here it is. Shut up and believe Him, stop over-thinking it and just accept Him as He is, because He accepts you just as you are. He says, don't change a thing, you're perfect. Remember He's not interested in change but instead EXCHANGE, so here's some good news: relax, because the fact is, you can't "exchange" a thing anyway. But He can and will.

How much of the big picture are you seeing? Are your preconceived ideas about Him and yourself masking reality, reducing His truth down to more manageable pieces that fit your views?

Do you think He came to die for you so that one day you won't have to go to Hell but Heaven instead? If you think so, you would be correct, but you could also reach behind you and touch the narrow gate that you have just walked through.

"For the gate is small and the way is narrow that leads to life." ~**Matthew 7:14**

The written and living word says there is so much more for you. So much more of Him He longs to give you, so many things He wants to do with you and for you.

The world has reduced the good news down to an after death geographical (heaven or hell) mental discussion, if it accepts there is a loving God at all. The reality is simple, He came, lived, died and rose again for your freedom's sake. His original intention for you is still in the forefront of His mind. Freedom from hell and into heaven, yes, but so much more! He desires an intimate relationship with you. He longs to restore you to your original glory in Him, one you never knew existed. He has an insatiable appetite for your freedom and an unreasonable desire to make you free to be you.

What do you say? Why don't you say right now

that you're beautiful to Him, that you ravage His heart? That you're His favorite. Really!!! Right now... Out loud... And I don't care if you call yourself a saved (Christian) person or not, do it anyway. I know it sounds strange, and to some of you a little intimidating. Dare I say, weird? But we're talking about the person who has chosen to tie His happiness to yours, gave His life as a ransom for yours so you could be free. I mean, really free. Ask yourself, what would it look like if we really believed what He thinks about us, how He really feels about us? How would it change how we think, how we see and how we feel about ourselves and others?

In this book, you have read some of the low points and some of the high points of my life thus far. I can tell you that the lows were much lower and the highs much higher than I wrote. The fact is if He's willing and able to do it for me then He will do it for you. He can't help himself, He's so in love with you. Remember, many years ago I was literally standing on top of a Gideon Bible in that cheap, nasty motel room, cussing out God Almighty through my whiskey saturated breath. I am the man that stuck my finger in the face of the man (Richard) who would later become my best friend and mentor and I was ready to cuss him out too, but God wouldn't let me treat him that way. Now I am free by God's crazy unrelenting love for me. I don't know everything there is to learn about Him, I've got a long way to go, but one thing I know for sure is that He has no taste (thank God) because He loved and valued me even then. He's not as civilized as you would think. The typical "civilized Christian" wouldn't hang out with me for fifteen minutes back then, but He has never left. Instead, He laughs and sings with excitement over my future and calls me deeper, reminding me that "the impossible is NOTHING."

Broken man, FIXED.
Troy

Lord, thank you for allowing me to honor you in these pages. Thank you for letting me testify of your power and relentless love that defies all reasonable thinking. Thank you Lord for your singular uncivilized thoughts of love and freedom for me.

Your Son Troy.

Like us on Facebook at:
www.facebook.com/TheImpossibleIsNothingBook

And check us out at:
www.TheImpossibleIsNothing.com.

About The Author

Troy and his wife, Michelle, have five wonderful children, each following hard after God in their lives. Troy is a highly successful business owner in the Texas Hill Country. He currently serves as part of the core leadership team and occasional speaker at their church. They have led home groups, community outreaches and are continually counseling and mentoring both youth and adults to walk out their destinies. Part of their current desire is showing others what it looks like to be supernaturally normal in their everyday lives. Troy's passion is encouraging others to BELIEVE GOD, NOT JUST IN GOD. He has an amazing story that truly testifies of the redeeming power and awesome love of The Father. Troy walks in an anointing that reflects that the IMPOSSIBLE IS NOTHING for God.

Made in the USA
San Bernardino, CA
28 July 2014